Petworth

THE PEOPLE AND THE PLACE

Christopher Rowell

First published in 2012 by
The National Trust
Heelis
Kemble Drive
Swindon SN2 2NA
www.nationaltrust.org.uk

In association with
Scala Publishers Ltd
Northburgh House
10 Northburgh Street
London ECIV OAT
www.scalapublishers.com

ISBN 978-0-70780-420-0

Text edited by Oliver Garnett
Project managed by Clémence Jacquinet
Designed by Isambard Thomas
Printed in Spain

10 9 8 7 6 5 4 3 2 1

PHOTOGRAPHIC CREDITS

Bridgeman Art Library / British Library: 13

Jane Buck: 135 a and b, 143 a and b, by courtesy of Apollo Magazine

By kind permission of Lord Egremont: 62, 82, 90, 91, 93, 98, 108, 136, 154

English Heritage: 56

David Gentleman: 156

Macmillan Publishers: 97

National Gallery, London: 29

National Trust Images / Bill Batten: 63, 64, 79, 83, 85, 90, 106, 127, 130

National Trust Images / A.C. Cooper: 108

National Trust Images / Stuart Cox: back cover, 43, 65, 68, 87

National Trust Images / Andreas von Einsiedel: 4–5, 7, 31, 46, 55, 61, 76, 89, 92, 99, 106, 126 a and b, 128, 129

National Trust Images / Andrew Fetherston: 48

National Trust Images / John Hammond: 10, 15, 26, 36, 45, 51, 52, 62, 66, 73, 82, 86, 91, 93, 96, 111, 118, 123, 124, 125, 132, 133, 136, 138, 139, 141, 142

National Trust Images / Matthew Hollow: 38, 39, 103

National Trust Images / Mike Howarth: 151

National Trust Images / Christopher Hurst: 42, 117

National Trust Images / David Levenson: 146, 147, 149

National Trust Images / John Miller: 145

National Trust Images / David Sellman: FRONT COVER

National Trust Images / Arnhel de Serra: 37

National Trust Images / Rupert Truman: 40, 44, 150

National Trust Images / Derrick E. Witty: 8, 14, 17, 18, 21, 23, 24, 27, 28, 30, 33, 35, 45, 57, 109, 110, 112

Tate Images: 77, 78, 80, 84 a and b, 113, 114, 120, 144

West Sussex Record Office / Garland Collection: 94

ACKNOWLEDGEMENTS

This book owes much to three colleagues: the late Gervase Jackson-Stops, the Trust's Architectural Historian (1975–95), the late Bobby St. John Gore, Adviser on Pictures and Historic Buildings Secretary (1956–86), and Alastair Laing, Curator of Pictures and Sculpture (1986–). Their written contributions on Petworth are set out in the bibliography. For help with this book, I am particularly indebted to Alastair Laing, whose comments and written contributions, both to the text and to the notes, are too numerous to be acknowledged individually. I do so here with many thanks. Alastair and I also worked closely with Lord and Lady Egremont, and Alec Cobbe, during the decade of works at Petworth (1992–2002), when the display of the public rooms was transformed in the spirit of Turner's Petworth, with the advice of the National Trust's Arts Panel. Particular thanks are also due to Sophie Chessum, who helped me enormously with research on several publications listed in the bibliography, most notably the *Turner at Petworth* exhibition catalogue, written and published in association with Tate Britain (2002). David Blayney Brown and Ian Warrell, my collaborators on that catalogue, provided many insights on Turner and his friends and their love of Petworth, as did Andrew Wilton. Numerous other colleagues, scholars and volunteers have contributed over the years to our present knowledge of Petworth, on which research is ever continuing due to the richness of the collection and to the magnitude of the archive, which reaches back to the Middle Ages.
The Petworth House Archives are owned by Lord Egremont, whose generosity and kindness in allowing scholarly access I once more acknowledge with much gratitude. Alison McCann, Archivist at the West Sussex Record Office, administers the Petworth Archives and is a fountain of knowledge on all aspects of the nearly 900 years of family occupation of Petworth. My great indebtedness to her is of many years' standing. In writing this book, which is based on my guidebook to Petworth, first published in 1997, I again pay tribute to Oliver Garnett, the National Trust's Property Publisher, for his help, advice and editing. I am also grateful to Clémence Jacquinet for her editorial assistance and to Andrew Loukes for help at Petworth.

[previous page]
The South Corridor in the North Gallery

'That house of art'

Limewood carvings of string and wind instruments, music and medals, *c.*1692, by Grinling Gibbons (1648–1721). (Carved Room)

The painter John Constable called Petworth 'that house of art',[1] and it still contains the National Trust's finest collection of pictures and sculpture. Petworth is also notable for furniture, woodwork, ceramics, silver, textiles and books, while its setting – which inspired Turner above all – is one of Britain's most beautiful man-made landscapes. First a fortified manor, then a palace, Petworth has stood for nearly 900 years as the seat of the Percys, Seymours and Wyndhams adjacent to the town of Petworth and at the centre of an agricultural estate. As well as being benevolent and innovative landlords, the owners of Petworth have often played significant roles on the national stage.

Petworth has passed by inheritance since 1150, when it came into the Percy family. The history of the Percy dynasty is a chronicle of power leading not only to high honours (the earldom of Northumberland in 1377), but also to death and dishonour. The Percy castle was repaired and extended by the 8th, 9th and 10th Earls of Northumberland in the late 16th and early 17th centuries. The 9th Earl was a notable scholar and bibliophile, whose son, the 10th Earl, a friend and patron of Van Dyck, founded the Petworth picture collection in the 1630s.

The 10th Earl's granddaughter, Elizabeth, as the Percy heiress, was married in 1682 to Charles Seymour, 6th Duke of Somerset, who rebuilt Petworth with her money. Nicknamed the 'Proud Duke', he looked to Versailles as the inspiration of the present palace, which was probably designed by Daniel Marot and was largely completed by 1702. A patron (most notably of Grinling Gibbons) and a collector, the duke employed royal craftsmen in the rebuilding and refurnishing of Petworth. His formal gardens, laid out by the royal gardener George London, were replaced in the 1750s by one of Lancelot 'Capability' Brown's most poetic 'natural' landscapes, immortalised in Turner's paintings. Brown's employer, Charles Wyndham, 2nd Earl of Egremont, inherited Petworth through his mother (a daughter of the Proud Duke). His collection of

***George O'Brien Wyndham, 3rd Earl of Egremont* by Thomas Phillips (1770–1845), 1839.** Oil on canvas, 187 x 155 cm (no.695; North Gallery)

Old Master pictures was displayed at Egremont House, Piccadilly, and most of his antique statuary at Petworth. The 2nd Earl was also a prominent Whig politician, serving as the equivalent of Foreign Secretary from 1762 till his untimely death in 1763.

Then began what has been called Petworth's golden age – the 74-year reign of the 2nd Earl's son, George O'Brien Wyndham, 3rd Earl of Egremont. A great agriculturalist, philanthropist and one of the most successful racehorse owners in the history of the turf, the benevolent and enigmatic 3rd Earl is famous as the host to a whole generation of British artists. A multitude of paintings and sculptures by Turner and his contemporaries remains as a testament to the 3rd Earl's generosity as a patron. He extended his father's North Gallery twice between 1824 and 1827 as the collection grew. Almost every room was altered and continuously rearranged in a restless search for perfection that culminated in his enlargement and elaboration of Grinling Gibbons's Carved Room.

After the 3rd Earl's death in 1837, his natural son, George, made few changes and was created Lord Leconfield in 1859. His son, Henry, 2nd Lord Leconfield, commissioned Anthony Salvin to make considerable alterations, principally at the south end of the house and in the Carved Room. In 1947 Charles, 3rd Lord Leconfield, gave the house and park with an endowment to the National Trust, thus ensuring their permanent preservation. The 3rd Lord Leconfield's nephew and heir, John Wyndham, offered a large proportion of the contents to the Treasury in lieu of the tax payable on his uncle's death in 1952, thus founding the Acceptance in Lieu (AIL) scheme, which continues to protect country house collections from dispersal. Wyndham was created Lord Egremont in 1963 for his services as Harold Macmillan's private secretary, and in 1967 succeeded his father as 6th Lord Leconfield. His son, Max, 2nd Lord Egremont and 7th Lord Leconfield, lives at Petworth with his family.

In 1992, with the collaboration of Lord and Lady Egremont, who have generously loaned numerous pictures, and with the benefit of an anonymous donation from one of its most considerable benefactors, the National Trust embarked upon the redecoration and rearrangement of the state rooms following extensive research into their history. The culmination of a decade of work was marked by the reconstruction of the 3rd Earl's Carved Room, whose re-opening in 2002, with the Turner landscapes commissioned for the room about 1828–30 once again *in situ*, was marked by *Turner at Petworth*, a special exhibition and catalogue produced in partnership with Tate Britain.

I

Petworth and the Percy family (1150–1632)

The Chapel, begun *c.*1300, looking west. The most substantial survival of medieval Petworth, it was refitted in the 1690s by the 6th Duke of Somerset, who installed the plaster ceiling, the stalls, urns and the private gallery above, surmounted in Italian Baroque style with vigorous carvings of curtains, angels and armorials

A 15th-century family tree in the Petworth archives traces the ancestry of the Percys to Adam and Eve via a colourful route that embraces the mythical Welsh King Vortigern and Brutus, the assassin of Julius Caesar.[2] For a distinguished Norman family of indubitable antiquity such claims must even then have seemed redundant. After the Conquest, the stronghold of the Percys (originally 'Perci') was in the north of England, and until the late 16th century Petworth was an outpost of their empire. 'The North knows no prince but a Percy' was a popular saying indicative of the feudal sway of one of England's foremost dynasties. The turbulent history of the family inspired Shakespeare and is worthy of the romances of Sir Walter Scott.

Until the 17th century, Petworth remained a fortified manor house, whose early 14th-century chapel is most evocative of its medieval origins. Its close location to the town of Petworth was typical of the time (the castle serving as a place of refuge for the inhabitants) and Petworth's gradual aggrandisement on the same site has retained its municipal links. The manor house, crenellated by royal sanction in 1309, stood at the centre of the Honour of Petworth, the great estate which was the gift of Queen Adeliza, consort of Henry I, to her brother Josceline of Louvain on his marriage in 1150 to Agnes, the Percy heiress.

The Percy estates were spread over eight counties in England and Wales, and although the Percys took their principal title from Northumberland (a barony and, from 1377, an earldom), most of their land was in Yorkshire. Topcliffe, Tadcaster, Spofforth and Leconfield (the last two castles were also crenellated in 1309) were acquired in the two centuries after 1066, and Wressell was added in 1380. In 1582 the net Yorkshire rentals accounted for £1,177 from a total land income of £3,602. The Northumberland estates – Alnwick, Langley, Prudhoe, Newburn, Tynemouth and Warkworth – were worth £1,529 per annum, while Cumberland, Cockermouth and Egremont brought in £351 per annum. The Northumberland and Cumberland estates were

AN REVERA HABITABIT DEUS IN TERRA ECCE CÆLI IPSI & CÆLI CÆLORUM NON CAPIUNT TE QUANTO MINUS DOMUS HÆC QUAM ÆDIFICAVI

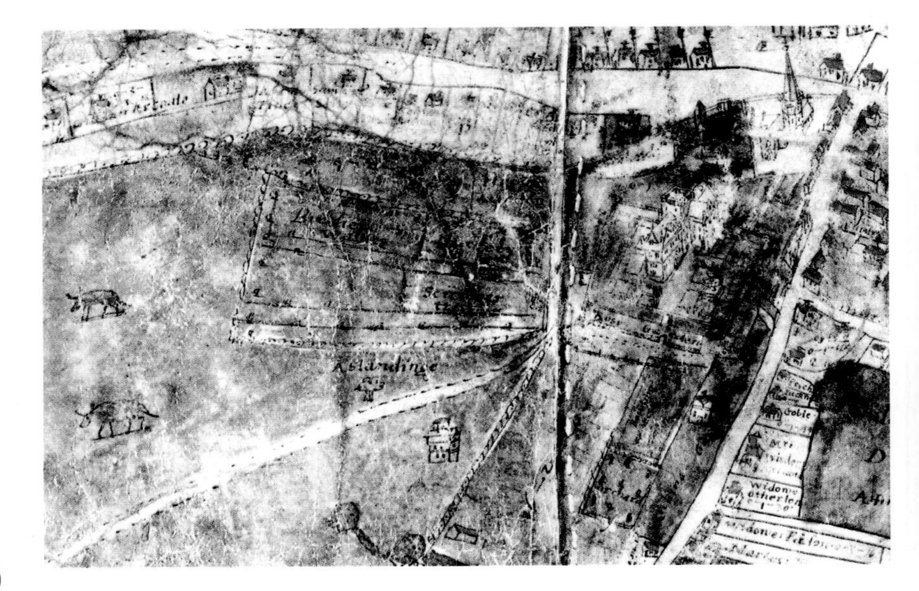

Map of 1610: *Survey of Petworth* (detail) by Ralph Treswell, 1610. Pen and wash on vellum. **This shows the old house and the 9th Earl's gardens, and the proximity of the house to the town and church.** (Petworth House Archives; Lord Egremont Collection)

largely acquired in the 14th century. The family's income from the 'South Parts' was much less, amounting to £582 per annum in 1582, and included (apart from Petworth) lands in South Wales, Somerset and Dorset.

Until 1576, when the 8th Earl of Northumberland was compelled to live at Petworth due to two previous attainders for high treason, the Percys, 'one of the greatest families of Christendom',[3] were based in the North. The Percy lion and crescent, still emblazoned at Petworth on fire-backs and furniture, but then also evident in hangings and tapestries, were potent symbols. The Percys' battle cry was 'Espérance Percy', adapted from the family motto 'Espérance en Dieu', which, like the lion and the crescent, adorned their military trappings. The feudal barony was granted by William the Conqueror in about 1066 to William de Percy. The 1st Baron, who had married Emma, a Saxon heiress of Semer, near Scarborough, died in 1096 near Jerusalem on the 1st Crusade. William de Percy's successors maintained both his close contact with the crown and his military prowess, being present (often with fatal results) at numerous battles in France, England, Wales and Scotland, including Bannockburn, Neville's Cross, Poitiers, Sluys, Crécy, Shrewsbury, Towton and the Spurs. The most celebrated was Sir Henry Percy, known as 'Hotspur', immortalised by Shakespeare in *Henry IV*, who was killed at Shrewsbury in 1403 in a vain attempt to wrest the crown from Henry IV. To dispel lingering doubts about his death, the traitor's body was exposed in the street, the head subsequently removed to a city gate at York, and the quarters hung above the gates of London, Bristol, Newcastle and Chester. A traitor's death was also the fate of Sir Thomas Percy, the 6th Earl of Northumberland's brother, who was beheaded in 1537 for his part in the northern Catholic rising known as the Pilgrimage of Grace; and of the 7th Earl in 1572, who affirmed his Catholic faith on the scaffold, after the failure of the Rising of the North against Elizabeth I.

Willing to risk all for power or for religion, the Percy family was a considerable political force in England throughout the Middle Ages and beyond, consolidating its position by a series of grand alliances, which are commemorated in the later heraldry of Petworth's chapel walls and windows. Norman French royalty and nobility are represented by such families as: de Brus, de Neville, de Balliol, Plantagenet, Fitzalan, de Clifford, Nevill, Lucy, Poynings and Fitzpaine. The fourth of the ten feudal Barons de Percy (by his marriage to Agnes) was Josceline de Louvain, through whom Petworth came into the family, and who was apparently handsome and skilful in tournaments. Richard, 7th Baron, was 'foremost among the sturdy barons who extorted the charter of English liberties from King John',[4] and Henry, 8th Baron, helped to negotiate the treaty between Henry III and the barons in 1264. In 1299 the 10th feudal Baron de Percy was created 1st Lord Percy of Alnwick, acquiring Alnwick Castle, subsequently the family's chief northern seat, in 1309. As a boy, his guardian had been Queen Eleanor of Castile, consort of Edward I, by whom he was knighted in 1296. He was captured at Bannockburn in 1314. His son fought in the naval action at Sluys in 1340, his grandson (the 3rd Baron) at Crécy in 1346, and his great-grandson (the 4th Baron) was present in 1356, as a boy of 14, at Poitiers. The last, a close companion (and later, the enemy) of John of Gaunt, was made Earl Marshal of England and 1st Earl of Northumberland in 1377. The remainder of his life was taken up with the great question of the succession to Richard II. Initially supporters of Henry IV, the Percys' subsequent rebellion ended in the death of Northumberland's son, Hotspur, at Shrewsbury. Northumberland was pardoned, but soon allied himself with the Scots against Henry IV, and was attainted in 1406. The Scottish invasion of England was halted in 1408 at Bramham Moor, where Northumberland was killed. His second marriage to Maud, daughter of Thomas Lord Lucy, brought Cockermouth and other Cumberland estates into the family. His successor, as 2nd Earl, was Hotspur's eldest son, Henry, whose titles and lands were restored in 1416, following the reversal of his grandfather's attainder. In 1455 he was killed on the Lancastrian side at the first battle of St Albans. His fourth son, the 3rd Earl, who was brought up with Henry VI, was embroiled, like his father, in the Wars of the Roses. He was killed, with his brother, at Towton (the bloodiest battle ever fought on English soil) in 1461, and his estates were confiscated. The 3rd Earl's son, the 4th Earl, had the estates restored by Edward IV in 1470, and in 1483 all the 1st Earl's estates before the attainder of 1406 were returned by Richard III, to whom the 4th Earl was Lord Great Chamberlain. After Richard's death at Bosworth in 1485, Northumberland switched his allegiance to Henry VII and became the Tudor king's main representative in the North. He was killed at Topcliffe in 1489 by a mob protesting about high taxes, and was succeeded by Henry, his 12-year-old eldest son. The 4th Earl had been a patron of John Skelton, the poet laureate, who lamented his demise in verse:

Richard II receiving Henry, Lord Percy of Alnwick, 1st Earl of Northumberland (1341–1408), at Conway, from Jean Creton, *La Prinse et mort du roy Richart* (Book of the Capture and Death of King Richard II), Paris, *c.*1401–05. Vellum, 28 x 10.5 cm. (British Library, Harley 1319)

What man remembryng howe shamfully he was slaine
From bitter weping himself can constrain?[5]

The splendour of the 5th Earl's establishment is commemorated in a classic document entitled 'The Book of all the Directions and Orders for Keeping of my Lord's Household Yearly', which was published in 1770

[left]
***Henry VIII*, studio of Hans Holbein (1497/8–1543).** Oil on panel, 238.3 x 122 cm (no.135; Carved Room)

[right]
Embroidered armorial panel, probably for a cushion, English, late 16th-century. Traditionally said to have been made by Lady Jane Grey (1536/7–54), but in fact probably made for Robert Dudley, 1st Earl of Leicester (1532/3–88) as it is emblazoned with his sixteen quarterings. Linen, embroidered with silk, wool and metallic thread, 43 x 60 cm (North Gallery)

as the 'Northumberland Household Book'. Because the family resided mainly in the North, Petworth is not included, but the regulation of the principal seats at Wressell, Topcliffe, Leconfield and Alnwick is described in detail, as well as that of the town houses in York and London. The Earl of Northumberland's household was modelled on that of the court and each grade, rank and function of his servants is described with military precision. This close attendance to domestic economy is indicative of an increasingly civilised and luxurious aristocratic way of life following the accession of Henry VIII in 1509.

From his earliest youth, the 5th Earl of Northumberland was famous for the magnificence of both his apparel and his retinue (which included his own heralds). Like Henry VIII, he was exceptional for his learning and wrote poetry. The timetable of his day was similar to that of his Norman ancestors: mass was performed at six o'clock (a choir was on the payroll), breakfast at seven, dinner at ten and supper at four. At Leconfield, the castle gates were closed at nine. Here, the sparsely furnished principal rooms were inscribed with verse by the earl's poets, Skelton and Lydgate. The earl's way of life was regal (he was known as 'The Magnificent') and peripatetic between his castles. In medieval fashion, hangings and portable furniture were carried from place to place. At this date English life still compared poorly with the elegance of High Renaissance Italy, Spain and France. None the less, the 5th Earl was one of the principal ornaments at the Field of Cloth of Gold in 1520, when Henry VIII met François I, and when Northumberland's retinue included 'twenty horses all caparisoned in trappings, of velvet embroidered in gold and silver'.[6] In 1526 Henry VIII visited Petworth, where he had 'good game and recreation'.[7] Northumberland's extravagance debilitated the estates. From a total annual income of £2,300 his domestic expenditure was approximately £1,500, leaving a comparatively small margin. In 1516 he fell foul of Thomas Wolsey, then Archbishop of York, and was fined £10,000. Wolsey's persecution of the old nobility was one of the factors that caused Northumberland's gradual withdrawal from military and state affairs. His son, the 6th Earl, who succeeded in 1527, not only inherited his father's debts but compounded them by bad management. Nor was he a natural soldier, despite inheriting his family's traditional role as scourge of the Scottish borders. He had the misfortune to fall in love with Anne Boleyn, which complicated his relations with Cardinal Wolsey and the king. Condemned to a loveless and indigent marriage, he was dogged by illness. In 1531 his debts led him to offer Petworth to the Treasury. His brother and heir, Thomas Percy, was executed and attainted following his part in the Pilgrimage of Grace in 1537. Later that year, the 6th Earl himself died, having bequeathed his estates to Henry VIII.

It was not until 1557 that the 7th Earl succeeded to the title, due to his father Thomas's attainder. Although his Catholicism debarred him from office under Elizabeth I, in 1563 he entertained the Queen at Petworth, where he was encouraged to live because of suspicions about his loyalty. Indeed he viewed Mary, Queen of Scots as Elizabeth's rightful heir and fomented rebellion in the North following her imprisonment. In 1569 Northumberland and the other rebels fled to Scotland, where they were imprisoned. Three years later, he was handed over to the English government, was beheaded at York in 1572, and was beatified soon afterwards. Once more, the Percy estates were subject to attainder. The traitor's brother, Henry, 8th Earl, had spent 18 months imprisoned in the Tower and had been heavily fined on suspicion of conspiracy before Elizabeth I, keen to prolong his late brother's attainder so that the Crown could benefit from the Percy estate revenues, compelled him to live at Petworth from 1572 to 1576, when the earldom was, yet again, eventually restored. However, even after that date the earl was forbidden to travel north, despite the queen's favour of a royal visit to Petworth in 1583. The 8th Earl now seemed to have reverted to Catholicism (despite an earlier recantation) and was gradually drawn into the Catholic plots (led by Throckmorton and Babington) on behalf of Mary, Queen of Scots. Imprisoned once again in the Tower in 1584 on suspicion of treason, he was found shot dead 18 months later. The official cause of death was suicide (he may have wished to spare his family yet another attainder), but he was probably murdered.

Because the 8th Earl was forced to spend more time at Petworth than any of his ancestors, he made many improvements to the house. In 1574 the earl's officers surveyed the buildings, finding the main house essentially in good order, with old stone walls and brick battlements, but the outbuildings were in need of major repairs. Although no plans or elevations were made, the 1574 survey reveals that the house was 'T' shaped, with a Great Hall, Pantry and Buttery as the cross of the 'T' at the north end, roughly on the site of the present North Gallery. Side by side to the south were the Chapel and a 'Fair Room' (the present Red Room) leading to the Parlour (or principal withdrawing room) as the upright of the 'T' (where the Carved Room is now). To the east was the Chapel Court with the Great Kitchen on the far side (within the present Domestic Block). Petworth was comparatively small and could not have accommodated the full Percy household in its heyday (the 5th Earl had more than 160 servants in 1512). The 8th Earl

Thomas Percy, 7th Earl of Northumberland **(1528–72), English School, 1566.** Oil on canvas, 155 x 99 cm (no.501; North Gallery)

repaired the existing buildings, built 'new lodgings', renovated the Chapel (supplying the brass eagle lectern) and created a 'new garden' with walls and fountain at a total cost of approximately £4,500. Petworth's general appearance, with additions made by the 9th Earl, is shown in drawings of 1610 and 1625.

Despite his own secret Catholicism, the 8th Earl had brought up his eldest son, Henry, 9th Earl (1564–1632), as a Protestant and determined for his children 'wholly to bring them up in learning'.[8] After private tuition at Petworth, the 9th Earl was sent on a tour of France, Northern Italy and the Low Countries, finally settling in Paris whence he returned to England on hearing the news of his beloved father's mysterious death in the Tower. Initially, the 9th Earl indulged (as he put it) in 'hawks, hounds, horses, dice, cards, apparel, mistresses',[9] spending lavishly and being duped, as he later discovered, by his agents. In 1586 a 'check-roll' listed 58 members of his household, fewer than that of his predecessors, and far short of the 100 officers and servants recommended by a contemporary theorist for the entourage of an earl. At first, having inherited his father's servants, he recruited new ones: 'young, handsome, brave, swaggering, debauched, wild, abetting all my young desires', and in a few years he reckoned that he had lost £60–70,000 through extravagance and 'unadvisedly, in sales of woods, in demises of lands or sale'. Eventually he checked this headlong career into debt: 'I must confess I was forced to discard to the very kitchen boys before things could be settled as I wished.'[10]

The 9th Earl's *Advice to his Son* is a fascinating insight into the running of a great establishment, and the 9th Earl's voluminous accounts chart the intricacies of income and expenditure within the equivalent of a huge business. In such a household, with landowning responsibilities in many counties, 'men are gathered together from all the corners of the world'. Many of the 9th Earl's principal officers were drawn from old county families with a long tradition of service to the Percys, and this loyalty extended to the lower servants. According to the 9th Earl, the first principle of efficiency was 'to understand your own estate better than any of your officers'. By taking the trouble to do this, and by buying land around Petworth and elsewhere, he had more than

***Henry Percy, 9th Earl of Northumberland,* Netherlandish School, 1602.** Oil on canvas, 212 x 102 cm (no.509; Red Room)

doubled his territorial revenues by 1598, increasing his annual income from £3,000 to £6,650. By the 1620s, the net income had risen to £11,000, reaching nearly £13,000 by his death in 1632.

The 9th Earl was 'naturally a kind of inward and reserved man',[11] being afflicted with deafness. After his debauched and spendthrift early twenties and military service in the Low Countries, he embraced knowledge, 'this infinite worthy mistress'. He had ample opportunity to pursue his studies when, in 1605, he was sentenced to life imprisonment for alleged complicity in the Gunpowder Plot: his distant cousin and employee, Thomas Percy, who was one of the conspirators, had visited him the day the plot was revealed. He denied the charges ('the world knows that I am no Papist'), but was fined £30,000 (he paid £11,000 in 1613) and was imprisoned in the Tower of London until 1621. Although he had lost his freedom, there were compensations. He was lodged in luxurious and spacious apartments within the Martin Tower at the north-east corner of the fortress. He had access to gardens and a terrace walk, while his accommodation not only included a study, library, great chamber and dining rooms, but also quarters for his 20 servants, including his cook and his gentleman of horse. An average of £1,000 per annum was spent on wine and provisions, and he was allowed to make architectural improvements – one of his first acts was to install a still-house, both for the distillation of potable spirits and, presumably, for the prosecution of his scientific experiments. His fellow prisoner was Sir Walter Ralegh, who wrote his *History of the World* (1614) during his incarceration and who is said to have presented Northumberland with the earliest surviving English globe, made by Emery Molyneux in 1592 (North Gallery). He certainly encouraged the 9th Earl's addiction to tobacco.

Northumberland had three principal scholars – the so-called 'Three Magi' – in his service: Thomas Harriott (1560–1621), the American traveller, the correspondent of Kepler on optics, a mathematician and astronomer; Walter Warner (1550–1636), an expert on algebra, who had the care of the earl's library;[12] and Robert Hues (1553–1632), a pioneering astronomer and scientific geographer, who had undertaken a world voyage between 1586 and 1588. 'Their prison was an academy where their thoughts were elevated above the common cares of life',[13] wrote a contemporary. The 9th Earl's reputation as a scientist, astrologer and alchemist earned him the sobriquet 'The Wizard Earl', but he was noted for other branches of knowledge, as the list of books dedicated to him reveals. These not only include works of arcane philosophical speculation, but also on such subjects as the breeding of horses (he encouraged the birth of horse-racing in the 1580s and built a great equestrian establishment at Petworth in the 1620s) and the building of forts (he had served as

***Henry Percy, 9th Earl of Northumberland* by Sir Anthony Van Dyck (1599–1641).** Oil on canvas, 137 x 120 cm (no.223; Square Dining Room). **This posthumous portrait commissioned by Van Dyck's generous patron, the 10th Earl, depicts the scholarly 'Wizard' Earl in a melancholy pose**

a volunteer in the Netherlands, commemorated in a portrait of 1602 and wrote a lengthy unpublished manuscript on the art of war).

The main source of information about the 9th Earl's interests is his library. Of the 826 printed books known to have been in his possession, 552 survive at Petworth (Lord Egremont Collection) and at Alnwick; he probably owned 1,250 volumes, a huge number at the time. He spent about £50 per annum on books, and his accounts include the names of several leading booksellers, including William Ponsonby, the publisher of Sidney's *Arcadia*. The books were usually bound in vellum, with silk ties, and stamped in gold with the Percy crescent within the motto of the Order of the Garter (which Northumberland received in 1593). Many are closely annotated with his observations, including works on mathematics, science, medicine, geography, history, military strategy, alchemy, sorcery and architecture. Works in Latin, French and Italian abound, encompassing literary classics as well as non-fiction. Although most of the books are now on open shelves in the White and Old Libraries, they were originally kept in chests within the 9th Earl's library at Petworth according to the inventory taken at his death. The library also contained 'one cupboard with mathematical instruments, one large globe and two small ones', and was hung with no fewer than 88 pictures, including a set of 24 Roman emperors (acquired in 1586) and a large picture 'of St. Lawrence'.[14]

While a prisoner, the 9th Earl contemplated a grandiose rebuilding of Petworth, to which he was confined after his release. 'The Computation of the New House at Petworth' (1615) reveals that this would have cost £25,000: a vast, but not impossible, sum based on £11,000 annual rental income. A ground plan, also of 1615, shows that the new house would have been built around courtyards, with a gallery of 315 feet running the full length of one of the ranges. In the event, he contented himself with merely extending the 8th Earl's house, but he did complete a huge stable courtyard between the present house and the lake. He had with him in the Tower his architectural library, including works by Vitruvius, Alberti, Serlio, Jacques I Androuet du Cerceau the Elder, Hans and Paul Vredeman de Vries, Scamozzi and Andrea Palladio. These, and his own experience of extensive building works at Syon in the early 1600s, would have fortified his dreams of reconstruction at Petworth. The 'pepper pot' lodges that he built at Syon, his house west of London, were to have been repeated at Petworth (but were never built). Their Neo-classical style indicates the influence of Italian and French architecture as well as its English interpretation by Inigo Jones.

The 1632 inventory of Petworth taken at the 9th Earl's death reveals much about the house and collection, listing every part in detail. A sign of great wealth and luxury is the large number of beds and seat

furniture covered with velvets and laced with costly *passementerie*, often *en suite*. The most important rooms were hung with tapestries, either 'imagerie' like the 'Story of Hester', 'forrest worke' (verdure tapestry), or 'herbadgery with halfe moones' (a combination of flowers and armorials). The 'Old Earle's Bedchamber' (the late 9th Earl) was hung with 'three large pieces of forrest worke with halfe moones [the Percy crest]' and furnished with well-used grand furniture including a blue bed with blue and yellow trimmings. In the several Wardrobe Rooms were similar textiles and tapestries, together with the Earl's Garter robes: 'St George his roabes'.[15] When the 10th Earl came to commission a portrait of his father from Van Dyck, it was entirely fitting that it should show the 9th Earl in academical robes and in a melancholic pose indicative of his love of study and of the acquisition of wisdom (no. 223; Square Dining Room).

2

The 10th Earl of Northumberland

***Algernon Percy, 10th Earl of Northumberland, and his first wife, Lady Anne Cecil* (detail) by Sir Anthony Van Dyck (1599–1641), *c*.1635.** Oil on canvas, 135 x 180 cm (no.289; Square Dining Room)

Algernon Percy, 10th Earl of Northumberland (1602–68), lived from the age of six with his tutor in the Tower of London until he went up to Cambridge in 1615. After 1619 he travelled widely in Holland, France and Italy primarily to learn the languages, as recommended by his father. He shared the artistic interests of Charles I's court, but prized the liberties of Parliament above royal absolutism. His relationship with Charles was complex. As a great nobleman of almost feudal stature and as a sophisticated connoisseur whose tastes were influenced by the example of Van Dyck, Northumberland had much in common with the king. As Admiral of the Fleet (1636–7), Lord High Admiral (1638–42), Commander of the Army in the second Scottish war (1639), and as a member of the Council, he was prominent in the king's government, while deploring the general unrest and bankruptcy caused by Charles's policies. As an energetic admiral, his proposed reforms of corrupt naval practices were shelved, although his ideas were later to be taken up by Samuel Pepys, Secretary of the Navy to Charles II. Northumberland's eventual defection from the king's cause in 1642 was deeply felt by Charles, who complained that he had raised Northumberland to office after office and had 'courted him as his mistress, and conversed with him as his friend, without the least intermission of all possible favour and kindness'.[16] Northumberland was critical of Charles's attempt to rule Parliament and although he did not wish to deny the king's prerogative, defended Parliament's laws, liberties and privileges.

During the Civil War, as a moderate Parliamentarian, he pursued a pacific line that earned both the respect and the suspicion of the two sides. He conducted Parliament's negotiations with the king, first at Oxford in 1642/3, at Uxbridge in 1645, and after the king's defeat, at Newport in 1648. He believed that the concessions made by Charles on the last occasion were sufficient, and wished to impose the same conditions on Charles II in 1660. He opposed both the King's execution

and the prosecution of the regicides. He took no further part in public life during the Commonwealth, and although he was given honorary court posts under Charles II, by then he felt himself 'too olde for the Gallantries of a young Court'.[17] Northumberland was termed 'the proudest man alive' by Clarendon, and 'was in all his deportment a very great man'. Clarendon continued: 'Though his notions were not large or deep, yet his temper and his reservedness in discourse, and his unrashness in speaking, got him the reputation of an able and wise man.'[18] Sir William Temple wrote to the 11th Earl, praising his father's 'great Virtues and Qualities'.[19] Sadly, the letter was written after the 11th Earl himself was already dead at Turin on his Grand Tour.

Despite his official responsibilities, his shortage of money (the Civil War is said to have cost him £42,000) and bouts of illness, the 10th Earl of Northumberland was active as a collector, patron and builder during the 1630s and subsequently. As a Parliamentarian, however indigent, he was well placed to acquire pictures from Royalist collections during the Civil War and the Commonwealth. Whereas his father had retired to Petworth after his imprisonment, and thereafter had not kept up a considerable London establishment, the 10th Earl first rented and then acquired palatial London houses as visible statements of his prestige. In the 1630s he rented Dorset House in Fleet Street and by 1640 was the tenant of the much grander York House, the palace of George Villiers, 1st Duke of Buckingham (1592–1628), whose magnificent collection was still *in situ* in the custody of Buckingham's widow and of the youthful 2nd Duke.

In 1642 Northumberland's second marriage to Elizabeth Howard, daughter of the 2nd Earl of Suffolk, allowed him to acquire Suffolk House, next door to York House, at Charing Cross. While modernising his new acquisition, Northumberland continued to live at York House (until 1647), revelling in the grandeur of Buckingham's pictures and sculpture, which included paintings by High Renaissance Italian artists, by Rubens and Van Dyck as well as classical statuary (purchased from Rubens) and Bernini's *Samson Slaying the Philistine* (Victoria & Albert Museum), which had been given by Charles I as the centrepiece of the garden. In 1629, while in England, Rubens had declared: 'When it comes to fine pictures by the hands of first-class masters, I have never seen such a large number in one place as in the royal palace [Whitehall,

[left]
***Charles I on Horseback (1600–49)*, Studio of Sir Anthony Van Dyck (1599–1641) and a later hand. Bought by the 10th Earl in 1645/6 from the possessor of part of Van Dyck's estate.**
212 x 120 cm (no.124; Carved Room)

[below]
The 10th Earl acquired Suffolk House near Charing Cross in London following his marriage to Elizabeth Howard in 1642. Drawing, *c.*1660, by Wenceslaus Hollar (1607–77, in the Pepysian Library, Magdalen College, Cambridge

close by Northumberland House] and in the gallery of the late Duke of Buckingham [i.e. at York House].'[20]

In 1645, at the height of the Civil War, Parliament voted to confiscate the Buckingham collection as the property of a Royalist (the 2nd Duke) and recommended that 'superstitious' (i.e. Papist) pictures should be burned. When it became evident that this would result in the loss of most of the £20,000 value of the collection, Northumberland succeeded in preventing the destruction. He also managed to acquire several highly important pictures for himself in consideration of £360 that was still owed to him by Parliament in recompense for losses suffered during the Civil War. As well as Titian's highly influential portrait of *Cardinal Georges d'Armagnac and his secretary Guillaume Philandrier* (Duke of Northumberland Collection, Alnwick Castle),[21] the paintings included several still at Petworth. By far the most important are the eight little paintings on silvered copperplates of Saints and Prophets, by Adam Elsheimer, which had already been detached from whatever piece of sacred furniture they, and some other paintings, had once adorned (nos.272–9; Somerset Room);[22] and two panels of the *Madonna and Child with Angels* (nos.320, 333; Lord Egremont Collection) ascribed to Andrea del Sarto (1486–1530). The latter of these – the so-called *Corsini Madonna* (no.333) – is fully autograph; both, ironically, were turned down by the Treasury in 1956 (neither is on public display).[23]

As a member of Charles I's inner circle, Northumberland's tastes combined architecture, the patronage of Van Dyck and the acquisition of Old Masters and antique statuary. With the exception of the king no other contemporary patron owned more pictures by Van Dyck, who had become Charles I's court painter in 1632, and whose expertise and profound knowledge of the arts was a considerable inspiration to Northumberland in the development of his own aesthetic interests.

The posthumous inventory of Northumberland House (previously Suffolk House), Syon House and Petworth lists 18 original Van Dycks and four copies.[24] There are 15 autograph Van Dycks and a further eight versions at Petworth today, most of which were commissioned or acquired by Northumberland, although the magnificent full-length portraits of Sir Robert and Lady Shirley (nos.96, 97; Red Room) came into the collection much later (before 1764). The 10th Earl's accounts reveal that he paid Van Dyck £200 for 'Pictures of his Lop. and Countesse and divers others' in 1635–6.[25] This must refer to the portrait of the earl, his first wife, Anne Cecil, and their daughter, Katherine (no.289; Square Dining Room), which, like the other double portrait of Lords Newport and Goring (no.300; Square Dining Room), was valued at £60 in 1671. The 1671 inventories also reveal that the average valuation of the three-quarter-length portraits was £30, and that the total valuation of Van Dycks (including copies) was £470. According to Bellori, Northumberland also commissioned from Van Dyck a now lost 'Crucifixion with five angels collecting the blood in five golden dishes, and beneath the Cross, the Virgin, St John and the Magdalen' – an almost unique instance of a religious painting done by Van Dyck for an English client, which the earl may have found it politic to dispose of under the Commonwealth (even though he was to own other – but non-contemporary – religious pictures). Northumberland's posts of Admiral and Lord High Admiral are commemorated in two portraits (both with nautical imagery, including prominent anchors) now belonging to the Duke of Northumberland.

At Petworth today is a series of three-quarter-length female portraits by Van Dyck, which were almost all in London in 1671, of Northumberland's relations, friends and connections. Although the paintings were acquired over a long period (partly by gift or bequest from the sitters, but also

Tobias and the Angel **by Adam Elsheimer (1578–1610), 1605.** Oil on silvered copper, 9 x 7 cm (nos.272–9; Somerset Room)

Catherine Bruce, Mrs William Murray **(d.1649) by Sir Anthony Van Dyck (1599–1641);** oil on canvas, 135.5 x 108 cm (no.295; Little Dining Room)

evidently by purchase), they represent a conscious emulation of the sets of portraits of famous or beautiful women that were formed on the Continent from the 15th century onwards. The nucleus of Van Dyck's cycle of beauties (four portraits of countesses) has hung in the White and Gold Room since at least 1764, when the majority of the Van Dycks were gathered together (as they are today) in the Van Dyck Room (now called the Little Dining Room) and the adjacent Square Dining Room. The Northumberland House/Petworth series may have been inspired by the similar group of Van Dyck portraits put together by Philip, 4th Lord Wharton, at Wooburn and later Upper Winchendon House, Buckinghamshire; its successors include Sir Peter Lely's series (*c.*1662–5) of court ladies painted for Anne Hyde, Duchess of York (Hampton Court), and the 6th Duke of Somerset's commission to Michael Dahl and Sir Godfrey Kneller of portraits of the ladies of Queen Anne's court (in the Beauty Room at Petworth).[26]

Northumberland subsequently commissioned similar portraits from Lely, who was able to study the Van Dycks at Northumberland House, and whose painting of the 10th Earl's daughter, *Lady Elizabeth Percy* (1648–9; no.524; Square Dining Room) is closely based on Van Dyck's depiction of the *Countess of Sunderland* (no.305; White and Gold Room, Lord Egremont Collection). In 1647 Northumberland commissioned

***The Younger Children of Charles I* by Sir Peter Lely (1618–80).** Oil on canvas, 198 x 231 cm (no.149; Somerset Room)

Lely to paint the portrait of *Charles I and his second son, the Duke of York (later James II)* (Duke of Northumberland Collection), and in 1649 Lely's poignant life-size portrait of the *Younger Children of Charles I* (no.149; Somerset Room) was transported from Hampton Court to Syon following the king's execution. It was probably painted at Syon, when the royal children were in Northumberland's custody, and was presumably hung in the king's apartments during his detention at Hampton Court. Lely's employment by the Percy family continued after the 10th Earl's death (13 portraits by Lely were listed in the 1671 inventory) and given that Lely assumed Van Dyck's mantle in the field of court portraiture, it is fitting that his work for Northumberland – and for his relations and political associates – should have helped to establish his position as Van Dyck's successor.

***Lady Elizabeth Percy, Countess of Essex (1636–1718)* by Sir Peter Lely (1618–80), *c.*1648;** Oil on canvas, 118 x 99 cm (no.524; Square Dining Room)

As well as transforming the English tradition of portraiture, Van Dyck was influential as a collector and connoisseur, having formed a superb collection of paintings by Titian. In the confusion that followed Van Dyck's early death at the age of 42 in 1641, Northumberland was at pains to keep track of the painter's collection as it passed into the hands of his widow's second husband and was then broken up to settle his debts. In 1646 Northumberland paid £200 to one of these debtors, Sir John Wittewronge (whose right to dispose of them was questionable), for two of Van Dyck's most important paintings by Titian: *The Vendramin Family* (National Gallery, London) and *Perseus and Andromeda* (Wallace Collection, London). In the 1671 inventory of Northumberland House, *The Vendramin Family* alone was valued at £1,000, almost a quarter of the value of the whole of Northumberland's collection, *Perseus and Andromeda* having been sold shortly after its purchase. That Northumberland felt some pangs of conscience about this *coup* is suggested by his payment of £80 in 1656 to Van Dyck's son-in-law, who then relinquished his claim to the two pictures. Northumberland had also acquired from Wittewronge, in exchange for several small pictures, Van Dyck's unfinished equestrian portrait of Charles I, which the artist had in his studio when he died (no.124; Carved Room).

Richard Symonds saw a further painting by Titian, 'A Venus lying along & Mars kissing her under a Tree & naturall paese franco', at Suffolk House in 1652. It used to be thought that this had suffered some damage, and that it could thus be identified with 'A naked Venus & a Satyr Done by Do. [Titian]' inventoried by Symon Stone at Northumberland House in 1671, which is now at Petworth (no.154) – and which was, indeed, begun as a *Venus and Mars*, as an X-ray had revealed. However, despite the identical subject, there are other discrepancies that make the Titian attribution doubtful. Meanwhile, a copy at Kingston Lacy (NT) of a miniature copy by Peter Oliver of the Earl of Arundel's version of the lost painting (Kunsthistorisches Museum, Vienna) has come to light.[27] At some point the 10th Earl must also have acquired the supposed Titians of 'A Persion Bride holding a little Catt in her Hands', later called 'Titian's daughter', that was

***The Vendramin Family*, by Titian (*c.*1488–1576) and workshop, begun about 1540–3, completed about 1550–60.** Oil on canvas, 206.1 x 288.5 cm. (National Gallery)

recorded at Northumberland House in 1671 (later one of the 13 pictures sold from Petworth in 1927, and destroyed by fire when in the Robert Guggenheim collection in Washington),[28] and both 'A Great Ecce Homo' and 'A Little Ecce Homo', of which there is no further trace. The early Titian of *An Unknown Man in a Black Plumed Hat* still at Petworth (no.298; Red Room) might, however, be identifiable with either one of the 'Two Men's: Pictures done to the wast, one by Jerjone, ye. other by Titian' appraised at Petworth by Stone in 1671.[29]

The 1671 inventories of Northumberland House, Petworth and Syon, which valued Northumberland's 167 pictures at £4,260 10s, indicate how they were distributed between his three principal southern seats (Alnwick Castle was excluded).[30] The majority of the best and most valuable paintings were, not surprisingly, kept in London, at a time when it was *de rigueur* to display one's principal works of art in the capital. At Northumberland House there were probably (i.e. allowing for several imprecise descriptions) about 20 Italian, 9 German, 35 Flemish, 6 English, 3 Spanish, 1 Dutch and 4 anonymous pictures (i.e. around 80 in total, valued at £3,282). At Petworth, there were 66 pictures, again with the emphasis on the Italian and Flemish schools, valued at £869. At Syon, there were only 21 pictures listed, mostly Dutch landscapes with a few, apparently Italian, paintings.

[above]
***An Unknown Man in a Black Plumed Hat* by Titian (1488/90–1576), *c.*1515–20.** Oil on canvas, 94 x 86 cm (no.298; Red Room)

[right]
Little Dining Room with, over the chimneypiece, Seghers's *St Sebastian* in its English 17th-century carved and silvered frame

The lists and appraisal of the pictures in the earl's houses was undertaken by Symon Stone, a painter of portraits, flower-pieces and copies, who acted as the curator of the collection from the 1640s until 1671. Connoisseurship was reasonably sophisticated in the circle of Charles I, so it is not surprising that Stone makes a clear distinction in the inventories between originals and copies, and sometimes expresses his uncertainty about an attribution. Stone's duties included helping 'to clense and ayre the pictures, keeping cleane the picture roome all the yeare', and he was paid 'for charcoles for ayring the roome'.[31] He received £8 4s 'for keeping the pictures at Northumberland House a yeare'[32] and was paid extra for crating pictures for transport (by boat to Syon), providing picture frames, undertaking restoration and painting copies of portraits and Old Masters for presentation to the earl's friends. He also acted as a cicerone and the fact that he was paid in 1666 for 'taking downe' and 'hanging up' pictures suggests that he was responsible for their display.[33] In effect, he fulfilled the same role as David Teniers for Archduke Leopold Wilhelm, who bought several of Charles I's pictures in the Commonwealth sales and whose Brussels picture gallery Teniers depicted in a series of paintings, one of which is at Petworth (dated 1651; no.76; Somerset Room).

The little we know of how the Northumberland collection was displayed has to be extrapolated from the 10th Earl's personal papers. Symon Stone was expressly charged with 'a picture roome', presumably at Northumberland House, and in 1637 Van Dyck's portrait of Strafford (1636; no.311; Little Dining Room) was hanging 'in one of the Galleries' at Syon. In 1657 payments for '11 ounces of greene silke string to hang up pictures' and '10 ounces red for lookeing glasses' imply that at least some of the pictures were hung on green and (probably) red backgrounds, both standard colours as a foil for paintings and known to have been used for this purpose at York House.[34] It is likely that the majority of Northumberland's pictures were deployed in galleries and rooms of state, with the smaller pictures perhaps gathered together in cabinet rooms or closets, just as they were in contemporary collections, e.g. at York House, Whitehall Palace and Ham House, Richmond (NT), where the Green Closet still exists. The accounts show that the pictures were framed in ebony or giltwood, a preponderance of ebony frames for both Northern and Italian pictures being typical of the time. Gerard Seghers's *St Sebastian* (no.601; Little Dining Room; Lord Egremont Collection), listed at Northumberland House in 1671, retains an ebonised and silvered carved frame which may date from the 10th Earl's lifetime, and several of the Petworth Van Dycks have gilt livery frames which may also date from the 1660s.[35]

Rare depictions of the somewhat earlier picture and sculpture galleries at Arundel House, The Strand, furnished with Italianate *sgabello* chairs of the same type that survive at Petworth, appear in Mytens's portraits of the *2nd Earl and Countess of Arundel* (*c*.1618; National Portrait Gallery; on loan to Arundel Castle, West Sussex). Similar rooms, with classical detailing in the Italianate style of Inigo Jones, may well have been constructed by the 10th

Earl during his alterations to Northumberland House between 1642–9 and 1655–7. His architect was Edward Carter, Jones's successor as Surveyor of the King's Works, through whom several royal craftsmen were employed. By this time, the traffic in what is now Charing Cross and Northumberland Avenue was becoming much busier and noisier, and the 10th Earl moved the principal rooms from the front to the back, thus creating 'a new front towards the Gardens', which John Evelyn in 1658 thought was 'tollerable, were it not drowned by a too massive, and cloudy pair of stayers of stone, without any neate invention'.[36] The garden staircase, added in 1657, was designed by John Webb, who also remodelled many of the 1640s' interiors, in a more pronounced classical style, as his surviving drawings indicate. Concurrently, Webb was responsible for virtually rebuilding Syon, whose rich interiors of the 1630s and '40s were commissioned by the 10th Earl and luxuriously refurbished in the process. As at Arundel and York Houses and at Whitehall Palace, the gardens overlooking the river at Northumberland House were peopled with statues. In 1645–7, Northumberland had acquired bronze statuary from Windsor Castle but this was displaced in 1657–8, when six marble statues were placed upon painted wooden plinths in the terrace walk. These and other antique marble busts and statues had been in Charles I's collection and were returned to the Crown by Northumberland in 1660. It is possible, however, that the Petworth collection may still contain antique statuary acquired by the 10th Earl.

The 10th Earl also made extensive alterations to the gardens at Syon and Petworth. At the former, he employed a 'French gardener', possibly André Mollet, in 1639–40, and his principal alterations to Petworth, conducted in the 1630s, also related to both the house and its surroundings. For more than 30 years, at all three of his principal southern seats, the 10th Earl was concerned with the display of his collections. As we have seen, Northumberland House was the principal repository of works of art, but Petworth (rather than Syon) contained a similar mixture of pictures, although in general of lesser quality. At Petworth, between 1632 and 1634, the 10th Earl spent at least £4,500 on repairs and building work as well as on furnishings that included tapestries worth more than £1,000, four beds 'with chayres, stooles and ffurniture suitable', and 'carpettes of turkey worke'.

The 10th Earl's architectural patronage was considerable and was largely extended to royal architects and craftsmen, but little remains because Northumberland House (demolished), Syon and Petworth were transformed in the late 17th and 18th centuries. None the less, the 10th Earl's patronage of Van Dyck and his collection of Old Masters produced a tangible bequest. His interests embraced all the arts. He bought 'cheny plate' (i.e. Chinese porcelain) in 1644–5, and one of the

***Josceline Percy, 11th Earl of Northumberland*; attributed to Sir Peter Lely (1618–80).** Oil on canvas, 134 x 108 cm (no.536; Square Dining Room)

greatest Dutch silversmiths, Christian van Vianen, supplied him with crested silver plate in *c.*1636–42 (a salver and covered bowl survive in the Duke of Northumberland's collection). His interest in contemporary fashion continued throughout his life.

The 10th Earl had followed his own father's example in taking particular trouble over the education of his heir, Josceline, Lord Percy, born in 1644 at York House. John Evelyn thought that, as a result, the 10th Earl had given 'a citizen to his country'. 'It is not enough', wrote Evelyn, 'that persons of my Lord Percy's quality be taught to dance and to ride, to speak languages and weare his cloathes with a good grace (which are the verie shells of travail); but besides all these that he know men, customs, courts and disciplines, and whatsoever superior excellencies the places afford, befitting a person of birth and noble impressions.'[37] In 1670, two years after the death of his father, the 11th Earl set out for Italy with his pregnant Countess and their daughter. They were accompanied by the philosopher John Locke, who was travelling as their physician. Lady Northumberland was detained by illness in Paris, while her husband pressed on to Turin, where he died on 21 May 1670, having over-exerted himself in the heat by travelling post for days on end. A few weeks later, his widow gave birth to a still-born son (another infant son had died in 1669). The earldom of Northumberland and the other Percy honours were now extinct, but the 11th Earl's three-year-old daughter, Elizabeth, inherited his ancestral estates.

3

The Proud Duke and the rebuilding of Petworth

The Grand Staircase, with Louis Laguerre's mural (*c.*1718–20) in the background

The Percy inheritance brought Lady Elizabeth many years of misery. Her widowed mother having married Ralph Montagu (later 1st Duke of Montagu) in 1673, she became the ward of her grandmother, Lady Elizabeth Howard, the widowed second wife of the 10th Earl of Northumberland (m.1642). The Dowager Lady Northumberland's grand plans for her ward embroiled them both in a series of disgraceful incidents. In 1679, when Lady Elizabeth Percy was 12, she was married to the 17-year-old Henry Cavendish, Earl of Ogle, heir to the 2nd Duke of Newcastle-upon-Tyne, a Tory who was later to oppose the accession of William III. Lord Ogle has usually received a bad press. He was certainly described by one of his young bride's relations as 'the sadest creature of all kindes that could have bine founde fit to be named for my Lady Percy, as ugly as anything young can be'. However, he was also said to have 'a quick and ready understanding' and to be 'a marvellous brisk forwardly young man'.[38] He died the following year on a Continental tour, his wife having returned to the schoolroom. Such was the glamour of the young widow (she had everything except good looks) that Charles II tried again to interest the Dowager Lady Northumberland in a match with his third son by the Duchess of Cleveland. This would have brought back the Northumberland title into the family, as the young man had been created Earl of Northumberland in 1674. However, the king was unable to raise enough money to satisfy Lady Elizabeth's grandmother, who also had no wish to marry her ward to a bastard, even a royal one. Instead, she was given in 1681 to an unsavoury rake, Thomas Thynne of Longleat, Wiltshire, nicknamed, 'Tom o' ten thousand' because of his great wealth. Having bribed Lady Northumberland, Thynne engineered the match against the wishes of Lady Elizabeth, who found him so repulsive that she soon fled to Holland. Before being forced into this unwelcome marriage, Lady Elizabeth had fallen in love with Count Karl von Königsmark, a colourful adventurer, with whom she took up again

The family pew in the Chapel Gallery: angels upholding the arms and coronet of the Proud Duke before festoon curtains, carved by the workshop of Grinling Gibbons (1648–1721) and John Selden (d.1715), and decorated by George Turnour in 1692, painted and gilded wood

after her escape to the Continent. Königsmark, a mercenary by profession, then instigated the murder of Thynne, who was returning home from an evening with his crony, the Duke of Monmouth. Königsmark was acquitted, perhaps by the intervention of Charles II, but his three paid assassins were hanged.

In 1682 the twice-widowed Lady Elizabeth at last formed a more suitable and lasting alliance with the 6th Duke of Somerset. Her former exploits (and her carrot red hair) were lampooned by Swift in 1711:

Beware of *Carrots* from Northumberland
Carrots sown *Thyn* a deep root may get,
If so they are in *Sommer set*
Their *Conyngs* [rabbits] *mark* them, for I have been told
They assassine when young and poison when old.[39]

Charles Seymour, 6th Duke of Somerset (1662–1748), known as the Proud Duke, has become something of a caricature due to the stories about his inordinate pride and pomposity. He corrected his second Duchess, Lady Charlotte Finch (his first wife having died in 1722), for over-familiarity (she had tapped him with her fan): 'Madam, my first Duchess was a Percy, and *she* never took such a liberty.'[40] (Lady Charlotte had been chosen sight unseen on the basis of coded reports by his chaplain, which described her as if she were a book. The Duke forgot his own code and had to get more explicit guidance from 'Beau' Nash, the famous Master of Ceremonies at Bath.) One of his daughters had the temerity to sit down in his presence (he had fallen asleep) and had £20,000 docked from her inheritance. A servant was dismissed for turning his back on the duke while using a bellows at the fire (a difficult operation to manage facing forwards). When travelling, the ways were cleared before the ducal carriage so that he would not be exposed to the gaze of the vulgar. On one occasion a swineherd refused to be moved away: 'I shall see him and my pig will see him too', he declared. In 1702 the then 42-year-old duke was described as 'of middle stature, well shaped, a very black complexion, a lover of musick and poetry; of good judgement but by reasons of great hesitation in his speech, wants expression'. According to the prejudiced Swift, of judgement he had 'not a grain, hardly common sense' and he was also said to have 'always acted more by humour than reason'.[41] Swift mentions his 'imperious manner' and he was 'humoursome, proud and capricious', according to another source.[42] Contemporary literature is full of anecdotes of his arrogance and of his inordinate pride. To Macaulay, he was a 'man in whom the pride of birth and rank amounted almost to a disease'.[43]

Perhaps he revelled in his ducal rank and royal lineage because his succession to the dukedom of Somerset was somewhat fortuitous. Until the premature death of the 3rd Duke in 1671, he had 'no more prospect of a dukedom than of the Crown itself'. His brother became the 5th Duke at the age of 17, on the death of his cousin in 1675, but was murdered in Italy by a jealous husband three years later. At this time, Charles Seymour was only 16 and probably at Trinity College, Cambridge, to which he was later to become a considerable donor as Chancellor of the University. Despite his brother's unfortunate demise, the new duke followed in his footsteps, and made a Grand Tour between 1679 and 1681. His marriage in 1682 to Lady Elizabeth Percy, the greatest heiress of the day, thus added to his high position the only element previously wanting: a large fortune. One of the conditions of his marriage was that he should change his surname from Seymour to Percy in honour of his wife's great inheritance. To his evident relief, his wife absolved him of this requirement when she came of age in 1688. Her majority was more significant in that it gave the duke full control of his wife's riches, thus allowing him to put in train (among other grand schemes) the transformation of Petworth into a ducal seat.

The Proud Duke was an energetic builder, patron, collector and benefactor as well as a prominent courtier and soldier. That Petworth was rebuilt in the style most closely associated with Louis XIV is indicative of the duke's absolutist tendencies, but also reveals the influence of his Francophile stepfather-in-law, Ralph Montagu, four

The west front, rebuilt (*c.*1688–1702) by the Proud Duke

[overleaf left]
***The Proud Duke: Charles Seymour, 6th Duke of Somerset* by John Closterman (1660–1711), 1692.** Oil on canvas, 207.5 x 144 cm (no.129; Carved Room)

[overleaf right]
***Elizabeth Percy, Duchess of Somerset with her son, Algernon, future 7th Duke* by John Closterman (1660–1711), *c.*1692.** Oil on canvas, 208 x 145 cm (no.127; Carved Room)

Charles Duke of Somerset

Elizabeth Lady Percy
Dutchess of Somerset
the Earl of Hertford

times Ambassador to the French Court between 1666 and 1678, whose London house in Bloomsbury (on the site of the British Museum) and whose country seat at Boughton, Northamptonshire, bear close similarities to Petworth. Montagu's French connections, Louis XIV's expulsion of the Huguenots in 1684, and William III's accession to the English throne in 1688 were three significant factors that brought French and Dutch designers and craftsmen into England and encouraged the spread of the Franco-Dutch Baroque style.

Both Montagu (probably) and William III (certainly) employed the Huguenot Daniel Marot, William's *dessinateur en chef*, whose style was widely promulgated throughout Northern Europe by means of engravings (for example of his interiors at Het Loo, William III's principal Dutch palace). Marot, who had previously worked for Louis XIV's *maître ornemaniste* (master designer) Jean Berain, is likely to have accompanied William III to England soon after his and Queen Mary's acceptance of the crown in February 1689. This would have allowed him to design the west front of Petworth (not completed until 1702) as well as the Marble Hall (largely finished in 1692). Elements of both are strongly comparable to Marot's work elsewhere, and the truncated central dome of the west front (destroyed by fire in 1714; rebuilt soon afterwards and subsequently removed in 1777–8) was also a feature of the façade of Montagu House, Bloomsbury (1686–8) and of the stable block at Boughton. The west front is also similar to Marot's De Voorst, near Zutphen, designed *c.*1692 for William III's favourite, the Earl of Albemarle, a friend and correspondent of the Proud Duke. If further proof of Marot's involvement at Petworth were required, then the Duke paid 'Mr Maro' £20 in 1693,[44] and 'Monsr. Marot' is also known to have borrowed a book from the ducal library. At Het Loo and De Voorst Marot collaborated with the Dutch architect, Jacob Roman, who introduced the 'circular roof' to Holland in about 1680, and this raises yet another possibility in the attribution of the west front.

Sculpture on Marot-esque plinths set between the ground and first floor windows of the west front

*Lady Elizabeth Percy, wife of Charles Seymour, 6th Duke of Somerset, riding in a triumphal chariot, c.*1718–20 (detail of Grand Staircase mural), by Louis Laguerre (1663–1721)

Comparison of the ground plan of the Proud Duke's Petworth, painted by Laguerre into his Grand Staircase murals, with the inventory taken in 1750 after the duke's death show how Petworth was arranged along Continental lines.[45] The principal rooms of state were laid out, as today, in *enfilade* along the west front overlooking the front courtyard and the formal gardens beyond. To the north of the Marble Hall were the public apartments, including the Carved Room, an adjoining Tapestry Room and a 'Picture Room next ye North Cloisters' (the present Red Room). To the south of the Marble Hall were the Dining Room (the present Beauty Room) and the principal bedroom apartment (incorporating the present White and Gold Room and White Library), called the 'King of Spain's Rooms' after the visit in 1703 of the future Emperor Charles VI, the then claimant to the Spanish throne. Adjacent, at the south end of the house, were the duke and duchess's separate private apartments; both provided a bedroom, with dressing room and closet. Upstairs, looking west, were additional bedroom apartments for distinguished guests as well as further family and senior servants' bedrooms. There were also first-floor North and South galleries, various wardrobe rooms, the 'Bathing Room' (with an adjoining bedchamber to relax in afterwards) and a 'Stool Room' provided with a 'Water Hole … Cistern and other Conveniences'.

The Franco-Dutch character of the Proud Duke's Petworth, which Horace Walpole described in 1749 as 'furnished exactly like Hampton Court',[46] was indeed carried through to the furniture and furnishings. Significant payments were made to suppliers of furnishing textiles and *passementerie*, such as Richard Alchorne & Co and Sir William Gostline.[47] The duke's accounts reveal payments to prominent French and Dutch furniture makers and upholsterers, many of whom also worked for the Royal Household, such as Gerrit Jensen, Jean Poictevin, Pierre Pavie and the carver, gilder and frame-maker, René Cousin. Unfortunately, no surviving piece at Petworth can be identified with any of the furniture described in the bills, but the house still contains superb examples that can be attributed to makers mentioned in the ducal accounts. The most magnificent furniture of this period listed in the inventory taken in 1750, two years after the duke's death, was richly upholstered, most notably the splendid silver-trimmed green velvet state bed, with matching window cornices and pelmets, in the King of Spain's Bedchamber. It must have been as sumptuous as the tall beds engraved by Marot, who is known to have provided 'a modell of the cornish' for a bed by Poictevin at Boughton. Perhaps Marot and

Two covered vases, *c.*1690. China, Kangxi period (1662–1722). Presumably acquired by the avid china collector, the Duchess of Somerset, wife of the 6th Duke, they stand before a contemporary Chinese lacquer screen, bought for Petworth at the 1882 Hamilton Palace sale and probably commissioned by the 4th Duke of Hamilton (1658–1712)

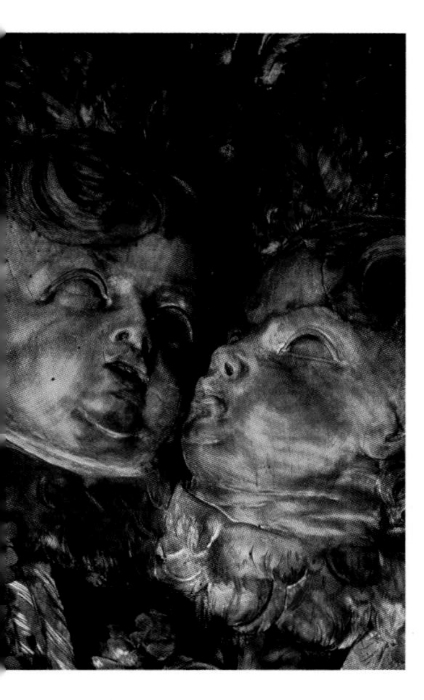

Carvings of cherubs, *c.*1692, by the workshop of Grinling Gibbons (1648–1721)

Poictevin (one of the suppliers to the Royal Wardrobe) also collaborated at Petworth. In 1686–7 disbursements included 'Upholstery vizt to Mr. Podvin [Poictevin] and Mr Robert Rhodes (besides £340 already paid) £50.'[48]

Like her friend Queen Mary, the Duchess of Somerset was an avid collector of blue-and-white Chinese porcelain imported by the Dutch East India Company. She paid several Dutch and English dealers for china, including 'Mrs Vanderhoven', 'Mr Van Collema', 'Mrs Bull for Delfe ware [Dutch Delft ware imitating Oriental porcelain]', while Mrs Harrison (who also supplied the queen) was paid £52 'for a Jappan Cabinet and frame' in 1695. There are numerous Oriental lacquer cabinets of this kind at Petworth: two 'India Cabinets' in the King of Spain's Drawing Room were each surmounted by no fewer than '22 pieces of China'. Profusion was an essential feature of such displays, as is evident from contemporary engravings by Marot and others, and in the duchess's China Closet at the private end of the house, glass panels over the door and chimneypiece were 'ornamented wth carved work & 45 pieces of China'. The reflections in the glass would have multiplied the effect of massed groups of china. This 'carved work' may have been by Grinling Gibbons, who supplied carved giltwood mirrors (two of which still survive) over the doors and chimneypieces of the Queen's Gallery at Kensington Palace (1691), which was originally ornamented with porcelain by Queen Mary. Another connection with the queen's method of displaying china is a rare set of carved walnut pedestals. They were designed to display large covered jars of Chinese blue-and-white porcelain. A set of similar, though plainer, stands survives at Hampton Court.

If Grinling Gibbons may have carved the duchess's mirrors, he was certainly responsible for the carved surrounds to the four full-length portraits in the Petworth Carved Room. Here, he created a room which, in its original guise, must have been all the more impressive for being half the size of the present one, which was extended by the 3rd Earl of Egremont in 1786–94. Gibbons's employment by the Duke of Somerset was almost certainly due to his previous work for the Crown. In the 1690s Gibbons worked at Trinity College, Cambridge, where he provided woodwork for Christopher Wren's Library, at the expense of the duke, who was Chancellor of the University of Cambridge from 1689 until his death. Gibbons's statue of the duke in the Wren Library (appropriately dressed as a Roman emperor) commemorates his generosity to Trinity. The quality of the woodcarving at Petworth is only equalled in Gibbons's *oeuvre* by the exquisite *trompe l'oeil* panel that he carved for the Grand Duke of Tuscany in 1682 (Uffizi, Florence), and a similar one in the Este Gallery at Modena. The Petworth carvings are all the more impressive for their much grander scale.

The central section of the west front, above the entrance to the Marble Hall: originally, there were statues on the parapet and a central dome

The Duke of Somerset also collected pictures and sculpture, although his contribution at Petworth is overshadowed by that of his predecessor, the 10th Earl of Northumberland, and that of his successors, the 2nd and 3rd Earls of Egremont. He was a friend of John, Lord Somers, a prolific collector of Italian drawings, and bought 'a case of prints' in 1706. Somerset was also a book collector, who is known to have acquired many of the books of Humphrey Dyson from the Chiswell sale of 1682, the date of the inventory of the Petworth library, which then contained 2,873 volumes.[49] He emulated the 10th Earl's collection of 'Beauties' by Van Dyck, and William III's set of whole-length 'Beauties' by Kneller, by commissioning a set of whole-length (subsequently rolled back to three-quarter-length on the orders of the 3rd Earl of Egremont) 'Beauties' by Michael Dahl, for a room that has ever since been named after them.[50]

His major acquisition as a collector was Claude's *Landscape with Jacob and Laban and his daughters* (no.329; Somerset Room). Claude's *Liber Veritatis* records two of his pictures having specifically been painted *per Angleterre* (nos.77 & 78, now in the National Galleries of Great Britain and Canada, respectively), which were probably the pair subsequently owned by Lely; and the 1671 inventory recorded, with quite a high valuation, 'A Landskipp Gloudilloraigne' at Petworth,[51] but the 6th

***Jane Temple, Countess of Portland (1672–1751)* by Michael Dahl (*c.*1659–1743),** 165 x 155 cm (no.195; Beauty Room)

Duke's is the first identifiable major painting by him to have entered an English collection, for which he paid in *c.*1686 what was then the huge sum of £200.

Richard Graham's regrettably lost 'book of notes of paintings Sold at several sales extracted from catalogues', as selectively recorded much later by George Vertue, lists the Duke of Somerset among 'buyers of pictures then' [i.e. up to Graham's sale in 1712],[52] but the duke's refusal to grant any lists of his own collection deprives us of the knowledge of what these may have been.[53]

In about 1710 the 2nd Duke of Argyll, on campaign with Marlborough, sent Somerset 'a modell Piece of painting lately come from Paris', which indicates that the duke's interest in pictures was well known. He also took care of the pictures he had inherited, employing Parry Walton in 1689–90 for 'lineing, cleansing, priming and packing 11 of Vandykes Pictures'.[54] Walton also supplied picture frames. In 1743 the diarist Jeremiah Milles, the antiquarian Dean of Exeter (1714–84), noted 'on ye backstairs, some very good pictures, to which the Duke in his whimsys will not allow a better place'. Of one 'incomparable piece', Milles 'could not learn ye name of ye painter nor ye history: ye former I am told ye Duke studiously conceals, as he does that of most of his pictures: out of an unusual and ridiculous whimsy'.[55] The duke's

***Landscape with Jacob and Laban and his Daughters* by Claude Gellée, known as Claude (1600–82), *c.*1654.** Oil on canvas, 143.5 x 252 cm (no.329; Somerset Room)

The Marble Hall: the original main entrance to the house was constructed by the Proud Duke in 1692, probably to the design of Daniel Marot, and still displays the duke's two full-length antique statues in the niches created to hold them. The ducal armorials above the chimneypiece were carved by John Selden

posthumous inventory reveals that he concentrated most of his pictures in what are now the Oak Staircase and the Red Room.

As he grew older, the duke grew ever more imperious, crotchety and eccentric. According to John Bromfield in a letter to Horace Walpole: 'One of his quirks was that, having survived all the servants that were possessed of accurate lists of the paintings [it being one of the duties – and sources of profit – for a housekeeper to show respectable visitors round a house], he refused to grant new lists, or copies, to the new servants, so that when he died half the portraits were quite unknown by the family; and the servants and agents of Duke Algernon, having on his accession to the title, etc., carried off all the papers that could be found, for purposes relative to their master's claim to the whole Percy estate; when they were reclaimed, on the Duke's death, no perfect list could be found among them by the next heir, the late [2nd] Earl of Egremont.'[56] This is borne out by the inventory taken after the death of the 2nd Earl of Egremont in 1764, and by the evident mistakes in the later inscribed or published identifications of sitters – especially of those in the Carved Room.

As for sculpture, the duke's most valuable acquisition (£108 in 1691) was 'a marble statue of the old Lord Arundell's beeing a Madonna with a dead Christ in her lap by Mich: Angelo',[57] a copy (Chapel Passage) of Michelangelo's so-called *Pietà* (St Peter's, Rome). Commissioned by the 2nd Earl of Arundel, it may be by Nicholas Stone the Younger (d.1647), who was employed by Arundel and is known to have admired this composition by Michelangelo. The two whole-length antique Roman statues in the niches of the Marble Hall (nos.56 and 57) are presumably the grandest surviving ducal purchases of sculpture as they are listed in the 1750 inventory.[58] The hall must have been partly designed around them in the spirit of a Roman atrium.

Several royal visits are recorded to ducal Petworth – including those of William III in 1693 and 1694–5[59] – but the best documented was that of 'Charles III, King of Spain', the English-backed unsuccessful claimant to the Spanish throne, *viz.* Archduke Charles of Austria (1685–1740), later the Holy Roman Emperor Charles VI (to whom the Proud Duke presented a gold watch by Tompion). On this occasion, soon after Christmas 1703, the other guests included Prince George of Denmark (consort of Queen Anne), and the 1st Duke of Marlborough. Prince George had taken 17 hours to come down from London, his coach having overturned twice. The guests being assembled on 28 December 1703, there followed a series of formalities worthy of Versailles, involving visits to each other's suites with colourful retinues. Here, of course, the Proud Duke was in his element. He took a prominent part in the funerals of Charles II, Mary, William III, Anne and George I and bore the orb at four coronations. He was Master of the Horse to Queen

Anne and George I. His familiarity with courtly ceremonial seems to have coloured his more than ducal daily routine. In 1743 Jeremiah Milles recorded that:

> The Duke spends most of his time here [i.e. at Petworth]: in grand retirement peculiar and agreeable only to himself. He comes down to breakfast at 8 of the clock in the morning in his full dress with his blue ribbon [of the Garter]: after breakfast he goes into his offices, scolds and bullys his servants and steward till diner time, then very formally hands his Duchess downstairs. His table, tho spread in a grand manner as if company was expected always consists of his own family the Duchess and his 2 daughters and when he has a mind to be gracious the chaplain is admitted. He treats all his country neighbours, and indeed everybody else, with such uncommon pride, and distance, that none of them visit Him.[60]

By this time, of course, he had long retired from public life, never in fact having regained his old position at court after 1715, when, disgusted with the imprisonment of his son-in-law, Sir William Wyndham (father of one of the duke's eventual heirs, his grandson, the 2nd Earl of

A copy of Michelangelo's so-called *Pietà* (St Peter's, Rome), which was bought by the Proud Duke for £108 in 1691. Marble, 119.5 cm high (no.125; Chapel Passage)

Egremont), on suspicion of Jacobitism, he instructed his servants to 'shoot all the rubbish' (i.e. his insignia as Master of the Horse) into the courtyard of St James's Palace. He was indeed far from servile as a courtier. In 1687, as Gentleman of the Bedchamber, he had lost his post but gained wide popularity for refusing the Catholic James II's order to introduce the Papal Nuncio at Windsor. Indeed, the duke's political convictions stemmed from his Protestantism. He encouraged the advent of William and Mary, was rewarded by Queen Anne for his early and influential support, and as she lay dying, took steps to ensure the Hanoverian succession. His political heyday was undoubtedly the reign of Queen Anne, whom his wife, 'a credit and an ornament to the Court', served as Groom of the Stole and Mistress of the Robes (in succession to the formidable Sarah, Duchess of Marlborough). Her tenure of office is commemorated in the Beauty Room by the portraits of the queen and of her court ladies.

The Proud Duke died in 1748 and was outlived by his son, the 7th Duke, for only two years. A soldier, who had served with distinction under Marlborough, the 7th Duke (then bearing the courtesy title of Marquess of Hertford) had in 1713 married Frances Thynne, a Lady of the Bedchamber to Queen Caroline, who aspired to the patronage of learning, entertaining the poets Thomson and Shenstone at Alnwick. When the 7th Duke died, having no surviving son, his property and titles were divided. He had persuaded King George II to grant him the earldoms of Northumberland and Egremont in 1749, with remainder to two of his male heirs. His daughter, Lady Elizabeth Seymour, inherited the barony of Percy; her husband, Sir Hugh Smithson, became the Earl of Northumberland, master of Alnwick, Syon and Northumberland House, and in 1766 Duke of Northumberland. The 7th Duke's remote cousin, Sir Edward Seymour, succeeded to the dukedom of Somerset but to the smallest portion of the property. Petworth and the earldom of Egremont devolved upon the 7th Duke's nephew, Charles Wyndham, 2nd Earl of Egremont, grandson of the Proud Duke.

4

The 2nd Earl of Egremont

***Charles Wyndham, 2nd Earl of Egremont* by William Hoare (1707–92), 1763.** Oil on canvas, 124 x 100 cm (no.538*; Somerset Room)

The Wyndhams come from Norfolk and are related to the Windhams of Felbrigg (NT). In the 16th century, one of the Norfolk Wyndhams married a cousin, of Orchard Wyndham in Somerset. In 1708 Sir William Wyndham, 3rd Bt, of Orchard Wyndham, married the 6th Duke of Somerset's younger daughter, Katherine, and thus it was that their son, Charles, inherited both the Egremont earldom and the Petworth estates on the death of his uncle, the 7th Duke of Somerset, in 1750.

Charles's father, Sir William, was a Tory who was briefly imprisoned in 1715 for raising a rebellion in the West Country in support of the Stuarts. He was freed by the intervention of his father-in-law, the Proud Duke. Sir William's political career had flourished in the previous reign. He was appointed Secretary at War (1712) and Chancellor of the Exchequer (1713), but after the death of Queen Anne in 1714, and his brief spell in the Tower, he spent the rest of his time in Parliament in opposition to the Whig government of Sir Robert Walpole. His mentor in public and private life was Lord Bolingbroke, virtually Prime Minister in 1714, but who, as an attainted Jacobite, never recovered his position after the queen's death. Sir William Wyndham, like Bolingbroke, combined considerable abilities with a love of pleasure. Both characteristics were passed on to his son Charles.

Sir Charles Wyndham, 4th Bt, later 2nd Earl of Egremont (1710–63), was first elected to Parliament (as a Tory, like his father) in 1725, but he came to prominence after his succession to the earldom, having by then allied himself with the Whigs. As 'the convert son of Sir William Wyndham', his political reputation increased to the point that in 1757 Earl Temple declared him destined to be another Pitt, whom he succeeded in 1762 as Secretary of State for the Southern Department (effectively one of two Foreign Secretaries). His principal contribution to foreign policy was to stand firm against the Bourbon alliance of France and Spain. At home, following the Marquess of Bute's retirement in

Pier-glass by James Whittle and Samuel Norman (*c*.1754–9). Giltwood, 426 cm high. **Pier-table, Italian, *c*.1730.** Giltwood with shaped white marble top, 85.5 x 187.5 x 75 cm (Red Room). **The pier-glass is the most splendid of a series supplied to the 2nd Earl by Whittle and Norman**

1763, Egremont's brother-in-law George Grenville succeeded him as premier, and he, Egremont and Halifax (the other Secretary of State) formed a triumvirate which was broken by Egremont's premature death in August 1763. Unlike his father, Egremont did not shine as an orator, but expressed himself admirably on paper. His French was impeccable. He first visited France as a young Grand Tourist in 1729, and the lure of Paris and *parisiennes* drew him back on several occasions. In 1736, the Francophile Lord Bolingbroke, in exile in France since 1715, extricated him from an entanglement with an actress. Egremont's enthusiasm for French style and culture was typical of the time, and is still evident at Petworth in the furniture and interior decoration that he commissioned, as well as in his activities as a collector of pictures and works of art, which are fundamental to Petworth's fame as a repository of the fine arts.

The goal of his Grand Tour in 1729–30 had, of course, been Italy, where he travelled in the company of the scholarly George Lyttelton, an author and a literary patron, who later became an innumerate Chancellor of the Exchequer. On coming into their respective inheritances, the friends distinguished themselves as builders, patrons and collectors. Just as Lyttelton in the late 1750s rebuilt and refurnished Hagley, Warwickshire, in the Rococo style, laying out the park in a Picturesque manner that even the ultra-critical Horace Walpole found faultless, so Lord Egremont made fashionable alterations at Petworth.

Egremont's aesthetic mentor was Thomas Coke, 1st Earl of Leicester (1697–1759). Indeed Leicester's family seat, Holkham Hall in Norfolk, is the key to much of the activity at Petworth and at Egremont House, Piccadilly, during the 2nd Earl of Egremont's 13-year reign. Designed by William Kent around 1730, Holkham was built (1734–64) as a setting for Leicester's collections and, like Egremont House, was still unfinished on its owner's death. The executant architect of Holkham was a local man, Matthew Brettingham, and this explains Brettingham's employment by the 2nd Earl at Petworth and in the construction of Egremont House. Brettingham's sculpture galleries at Holkham and Petworth are still strikingly similar, despite the extension of the latter in the 1820s.[61]

The craftsmen paid by Leicester also reappear in the 2nd Earl's accounts: Whittle and Norman, Vile and Cobb, Paul Saunders, William Bradshaw and William Hallett for furniture, picture frames, upholstery and tapestries; Maydwell and Windle for chandeliers and lustres; Thomas Bromwich for wallpapers; and Benjamin and Thomas Carter for chimneypieces. Brettingham's son, also Matthew, acted for both Leicester and Egremont as a purveyor of classical statuary. In partnership with the painter, archaeologist and dealer Gavin Hamilton, Brettingham the Younger bought antique statuary for Leicester between

1749 and 1754 and for Egremont between 1755 and 1763, thus creating two of the most important English collections to survive intact in their original settings (Petworth is the larger). If the sculpture formed an essential element of Holkham's interiors, so too did the pictures: 'I forgot to tell you', wrote Admiral Boscawen – the naval hero, an early patron of Robert Adam at Hatchlands Park (NT), and Egremont's fellow-guest at Holkham – to his wife in 1757, 'that Lord Leicester has a very fine collection of pictures, Lord Egremont who knows the hands and seems to understand them, says at least ten thousand pounds worth.'[62]

The first entry in Egremont's accounts to refer to a work of art was in 1735: 'paid Mr Hogarth the Painter £4:4:0', although only two rather second-rate copies after Hogarth remain at Petworth.[63] In 1740, the year of his father's death, the opening entry in his account book reveals that he then had £1,220 4s 6d in ready money, from which he paid £133 17s 6d 'for pictures and bronzes' at an auction. By 1741 he was buying 'tapestry fauteuils [armchairs] from Paris'[64] and he bought other French furniture, notably the Boulle marquetry desks flanking the chimneypiece in the Somerset Room, while paying cabinetmakers, upholsterers and upholders such as Hallett and Bradshaw. At this time, Egremont was making improvements at Whitham, his country house in Somerset, and at his London house in Greek Street, which was fitted up by the upholder and cabinetmaker, William Bradshaw. His expenditure in the 1740s reveals, albeit on a smaller scale, the varied interests that he was later to be able to indulge to the full. As a member (from 1742) of the Society of Dilettanti, founded in 1732 to prolong the civilised interests of those who had made the Grand Tour, he would have been abreast of the latest Italian developments in the antiquarian field. Lords Lyttelton and Leicester also belonged to this most cultivated of convivial societies. Payments for pictures – usually bought at auction or through dealers afterwards (e.g. the £94 6s paid out in 1742 after Lord Thomond's sale) and picture frames (by Gosset, Waters and Welbeloved) – predominate, although there are payments to silversmiths (Willaume, de Lamerie and Archambo), to china dealers and gardeners, as well as to furniture-makers and upholsterers such as Paul Saunders.

After acceding to Petworth and the earldom of Egremont in 1750, Charles was able to spread his wings. Indeed, his annual expenditure between October 1749 and December 1750 had already increased to £9,279, presumably in anticipation of his inheritance. The following year (1751) he spent the huge sum of £34,359, and until 1760 his annual outgoings were £10–18,000, with the exception of 1756 and 1757, when he spent £55,000 and £75,000, partly on his new London house. This indicates that he must have received much more than Horace Walpole's estimate of 'about £12,000 a year of the Percy estate'.[65] In 1751 he

The White and Gold Room, *c.*1755–61, designed by Matthew Brettingham the Elder, with stucco by Francesco Vassalli. Van Dyck's *Lady Anne Carr* hangs on the far wall above François Rübestück's desk, *c.*1780. The tapestry chairs, French *c.*1760, were bought in 1882 at the Hamilton Palace sale. The overmantel giltwood glass is one of the remarkable series attributed to Whittle and Norman, *c.*1754–9

married Alicia Carpenter, a noted beauty and daughter of an Irish peer, Lord Carpenter. On 21 February that year 'Hardel the Jeweller' received no less than £2,055 for 'the Diamond drops', no doubt an extravagant gift to his betrothed, and 'a set of Dresden China £40' may well have been bought with an eye to his marriage.[66] Having in 1750 paid £912 12s 4d 'for all the things at Petworth belonging to the late Duke of Somerset's estate',[67] his first major expenses there seem to have been connected with the garden.

The 2nd Earl had a passion for gardening: one of his first recorded payments was for 'fruit trees' in 1741, and he paid a Bath gardener for 'exoticks' in 1749. However, he is most famous for his patronage of Lancelot 'Capability' Brown, who was first consulted at Petworth in 1751 and who drew up his proposed design for the whole park in 1752. He also laid out the garden of Egremont House.

The 2nd Earl was less radical in his treatment of the house. Indeed, apart from his creation of the North Gallery, his only major alteration was the remodelling of the Rococo White and Gold Room, probably between 1755 and 1761, when the Italian-Swiss *stuccatore* Francesco Vassalli was paid for plasterwork. As the 1764 inventory reveals, the 2nd Earl largely refurnished Petworth and from 1750 was actively employing cabinetmakers, upholsterers and upholders, some of whom he had patronised in the 1740s for Whitham and Greek Street.[68] Chief among them was the fashionable and expensive firm of Whittle and Norman. When their London warehouse burned down in 1759, shortly after Whittle's death the same year, the firm suffered a major loss, including furniture commissioned by Egremont, but partly due to his continued patronage, Whittle and Norman recovered. Between 1760–3 most of the furniture and furnishings of Egremont House was provided by Samuel Norman.[69]

On the 7th Duke's death, Northumberland House in London had gone to the future Duke of Northumberland. The 2nd Earl of Egremont did not therefore inherit a town house with Petworth. His own house

Egremont House, Piccadilly, built 1756–63 by Matthew Brettingham the Elder for the 2nd Earl. Photograph (1885) by H. Bedford Lemere

in Greek Street had presumably been given up, because he was leasing a house in Whitehall from the Duke of Richmond when, in 1756, he bought a plot of land and adjacent buildings at the western end of Piccadilly overlooking Green Park. Here, Egremont House still stands, behind its walled courtyard (between 1865 and 1998, it housed the Naval and Military Club, called the 'In and Out' due to the signs on its gate piers). The new house, its plain Palladian façade in contrast to the riches within, was designed and built by Matthew Brettingham the Elder to provide for large numbers of guests and works of art, with a series of grand intercommunicating rooms arranged around a domed central staircase.

Concurrently, Brettingham was instructed to provide a sculpture gallery at Petworth – presumably due to lack of space on the London site and because the 2nd Earl was only just beginning to collect sculpture in 1756.

As in the 1671 inventory, the 1764 inventories following the 2nd Earl's early death reveal that the best pictures were displayed in London. Petworth contained chiefly inherited portraits, and Egremont House was the receptacle for over 200 Old Master pictures, including those inherited from the Northumberland House collection. Most of them had, however, been purchased by the earl himself. He bought at least one picture abroad, 'a little piece by Steenwyck', perhaps the *Christ with Nicodemus* (no.242; Somerset Room), which was acquired in Brussels or Antwerp in 1752. In 1759 Matthew Brettingham the Younger sent him 'eight Small Pictures from Italy', including landscapes by Vanvitelli and Locatelli. The 'Picture Book', in which he listed his purchases,[70] reveals that ten other pictures came from Rome, including a 'Madonna of Conca', and two more in 1761. However, most were bought on the burgeoning London art market, which was then beginning to challenge Amsterdam and Paris. Dealers such as Samuel Paris and 'Dr' Robert

Bragge regularly travelled on the Continent, imported pictures and sold them in London through auctioneers such as Langford and Prestage. These names occur often in the 2nd Earl's accounts as well as those of other dealers such as John Blackwood and the artist/dealer Arthur Pond. The earl bought at the break-up of notable collections including those of Sir Luke Schaub (1758) and Dr Meade (1754) and at the initial sale in 1751 of pictures from the late Sir Robert Walpole's collection at Houghton Hall, Norfolk, which the 2nd Earl visited several times. His connoisseurship seems to have been greater than the norm, but he presumably received advice from men like John Anderson, who certainly worked for him as a picture restorer and go-between.

Horace Walpole linked Lord Egremont with a group of rich collectors whose 'glaring extravagance is the constant high price given for pictures'.[71] The 2nd Earl's picture collection is one of the best documented of the mid 18th century and it is possible to establish that

***The Selling of Joseph* by Sébastien Bourdon (1616–71), *c*.1640.** Oil on canvas 87 x 112 (no.18; Red Room). **It was bought by the 2nd Earl in 1756 and is in the frame for which Samuel Norman probably charged four guineas in 1762**

***Card Players* by Jan Massys [Matsys] (*c.*1509–75).**
Oil on canvas, 73.5 x 101.5 cm (no.47; Red Room)

most of the prices were in fact reasonable.[72] Jean Barbault's *Dowered Young Woman* (no.520*; White and Gold Room; Lord Egremont Collection) cost under £5 in 1753; Ruisdael's *Waterfall* (no.48*; Somerset Room) cost less than £10; Horst's *Boys at Play* (no.572; Bedroom Corridor) was £21; and in 1760 he paid £24 for a large landscape, then attributed to Cuyp, but which is probably the picture now given to Abraham van Calraet (no.207; Somerset Room). More expensive were Bourdon's *Selling of Joseph* (no.18; Somerset Room) at £99 in 1756 and Bril's *Landscape* (no.83; Somerset Room), which cost £126 in 1754 and retains its magnificent French carved giltwood frame of *c.*1730.[73] The most expensive picture still in the collection is Teniers's *The Brussels Picture Gallery of the Archduke Leopold Wilhelm* – £241 in 1756 (no.76; Somerset Room). The most expensive of all, Maratta's *Martyrdom of St Andrew*, cost £273 in 1758, and was sold in 1794 for £298. It is interesting to compare these prices with the valuation of the 10th Earl's Titian, *The Vendramin Family*, at £1,000 in 1671, with the £200 paid by the Proud Duke for his Claude in 1683, and with the much larger sums paid to contemporary British artists by the 3rd Earl in the early 19th century. They should also be seen in the context of the 2nd Earl's total annual expenditure, which in normal years varied between £10,000 and £18,000, and against the £1,700 paid to Samuel Norman for the furnishing of Egremont House.

The 2nd Earl's taste was typical of his time, apart from, for example, his comparatively expensive purchase at £48 of Jan Massys's *Card Players* (no.47; Red Room) and 'Two Large Murillios from

Rotterdam' at just over £118 (when the Early Netherlandish and Spanish schools were generally not in favour). He was also in the vanguard of a revived taste for Dutch paintings. The entries in his 'Picture Book', beginning in 1748, reveal that he bought more than 180 pictures during the last fifteen years of his life. The 'Picture Book'[74] and the posthumous 1764 inventory of Egremont House reflect his priorities.[75] Half of them were Italian (mostly 16th–17th-century subject pictures, but including ruin or landscape scenes by contemporary artists such as Panini and Canaletto), a third was Dutch or Flemish and an eighth was French. Of the 220 pictures listed at Egremont House in 1764, 99 were Italian, 32 were Flemish, 35 Dutch, 24 French, eleven German, two Spanish and ten unattributed. Some were inherited, but the majority were the earl's own purchases.

***Lady Mary Dudley, Lady Sidney (d.1586)*, circle of Hans Eworth (*c.*1540–73).** Oil on canvas; 195.5 x 115.5 cm, (no.499; Somerset Room)

The 2nd Earl's posthumous inventory taken at Petworth[76] only gives the names of artists for some pictures (chiefly for those in rooms on the ground floor that visitors would have seen and for which there was, presumably, a housekeeper's list), and in other rooms simply gives a number and, generally, a location. 228 paintings are enumerated, of which 71 are identified as portraits.

As a patron, the 2nd Earl was conservative: he commissioned portraits in oils of himself and his wife, the Hon. Alicia Carpenter (nos.371, 538*), who was herself an amateur artist.[77] He also commissioned portraits of her from Gainsborough (no.100; Lord Egremont Collection) and Hoare of Bath,[78] but nothing from Reynolds. Nor did he buy or commission landscapes, sporting pictures, genre scenes, or history paintings, from English artists. However, he did have an interest in English painting of an earlier age. He acquired the portraits of *Sir Henry Sidney* and *Mary Dudley, Lady Sidney* (nos. 498, 499).[79] The latter incorporates the first illusionistic fly in English painting.

At Egremont House, the principal rooms, opulently furnished in the French style by Samuel Norman,[80] were filled with pictures, symmetrically arranged and hung by gilt metal rings from nails or from silk cords matching the crimson or blue Genoa damask wall-hangings, festoon curtains and upholstery. Samuel Norman's alterations to certain old frames and his provision of pairs and triads of matching frames (in one case copying 'an old

French frame') indicate that great care was taken to achieve balanced symmetrical arrangements, due emphasis being given to overmantels. Lighting was also considered. There were numerous torchère stands and the overmantel picture frame in the Blue Drawing Room had six candle sconces, perhaps inspired by similar picture frames incorporating candles at Norfolk House, built by Matthew Brettingham for the 9th Duke of Norfolk. There was some degree of thematic arrangement: the Dining Parlour contained the usual depictions of live and dead game, including Snyders's huge *Concert of Birds* (no.517; Oak Stairs) still in its ornate giltwood frame by Samuel Norman. Lord Egremont's Drawing Room was almost entirely devoted to landscapes (including Bril's *A Landscape*; no.83; Somerset Room) as well as the putative Titian *Nymph and Faun* (no.154; Somerset Room), perhaps in homage to the Landscape Room at Holkham. Otherwise, the pictures were a miscellany in terms of subject-matter and school, no concession being made to the function of the room. Thus 'My Lady's New Dressing Room' contained 48 pictures, including some very masculine subjects as well as Ruisdael's *Waterfall* (no.48*), Steenwyck's *Church* (no.389) and the eight little Elsheimers in Rococo frames supplied by Joseph Duffour in 1752 (all now in the Somerset Room). The 3rd Earl's sale in 1794 of Egremont House, most of its furniture and most of his father's pictures, broke up what was undoubtedly one of the most discriminating and beautifully arranged mid-18th-century collections.

More extraordinary than the 2nd Earl's purchase of nearly 200 paintings and his patronage of contemporary craftsmen is his achievement as a collector of antique sculpture. That his collection of some 70 statues and busts remains intact in the gallery that he built for it makes Petworth all the more remarkable. Antique sculpture was extremely expensive (the considerable cost of packing and transport had to be added to the purchase price), and its export was stringently controlled by the papacy, which built up its own pre-eminent collections, still magnificently housed in the Papal Museums within the Vatican. The Pope rarely gave licences for excavations within the Papal States, but certain dealers were allowed the privilege of digging in exchange for money and a share of the finds. It was also occasionally possible to acquire statues or other antiquities from the ancestral collections of the principal Italian families. One Italian collector, Cardinal Alessandro Albani, whose collections rivalled those of the Pope, was something of a *marchand-amateur* (dealer-collector), both acquiring and dealing within a complex and sophisticated circle, and at least one piece now at Petworth has an Albani provenance (no.18; North Gallery). Within Albani's orbit were also the two men who put together the 2nd Earl's collection: Gavin Hamilton and Matthew Brettingham the Younger, who regarded the 2nd Earl as their 'patron

***Agrippina as Ceres*, female portrait statue, Roman adaptation of a Greek original of the end of the 5th century BC, restored and published (1768–72) by Bartolomeo Cavaceppi (1716–99).** Parian marble, 193 cm high (no.3; North Gallery)

Seated Statue of a Man, **Roman, 2nd century AD, with 3rd century AD head of Emperor Gallienus.** Marble, 150 cm high (no.15; North Gallery). **Fixed into the early 19th-century plinth is a *Hero Relief*, Greek, 5th century BC.** Pentelic marble, 76 x 63 cm. (no.72; North Gallery)

and benefactor'. Hamilton was a portrait and history painter, who spent most of his time as a dealer, cicerone and excavator; Brettingham was, of course, the son of the 2nd Earl's architect. Their links with Albani were of paramount importance: not only did they find it easier to obtain papal licences for excavation and export, but they had access to the greatest expert of the day, Johann Winckelmann, who lived at Albani's villa on a pension that allowed him to write his *magnum opus* on antique sculpture, *Geschichte der Kunst des Alterthums* [*History of Ancient Art*], 1764. Another benefit, at a time when English collectors 'had no value for statues *without heads*',[81] was their ability to employ experienced restorers of excavated fragments, including Pietro Pacilli (1716–73) and Bartolomeo Cavaceppi (1716–99), the friend of Winckelmann, and Albani's principal restorer, whose published account of his work, the *Raccolta* (1768–72), includes engravings of two statues restored for 'Milord Egremont' still in the North Gallery (nos.1, 3).[82] The restorers' skill lay in joining together antique fragments with new elements to provide apparently complete figures, which would stand in symmetrical and harmonious ranks.

The sculpture galleries of northern collectors were closely based on Italian models, themselves founded upon the canons of ancient Roman and Greek architecture. Thus, although Brettingham's Petworth gallery is not as advanced in its design as, say, Adam's gallery at Newby Hall, Yorkshire (a top-lit rotunda directly modelled on the Pantheon), it is none the less reminiscent of the long rectangular galleries of Roman *palazzi* and museums, with statues in niches, or on plinths, and busts mounted on brackets within indented roundels, or placed on consoles. The Petworth gallery was formed by glazing an open cloister at the north end of the house, which in 1750 contained '4 Marble Tables on Walnuttree frames' and '6 broken Cane Chairs'. Such arcades or *loggias* were used as sculpture galleries by the ancient Romans and by their Italian successors. Its northern aspect was also entirely appropriate: Vitruvius himself had recommended a steady northern light as ideal for artists' studios and therefore by implication for the display of pictures and other works of art, and this was repeated by European theorists from the late 16th century. Brettingham's name first appears in the 2nd Earl's accounts in 1753. The '7 large Sash frames with Circular heads' were paid for in October 1754, which must mean that the structure had been completed earlier that year.

The first mention of an antiquity was on 11 March 1755, when the 2nd Earl paid £21 10s 6d for an antique bust of Isis at Dr Mead's sale. On 17 March Gavin Hamilton received £50 'for an antique bust of Venus' – possibly the 'Leconfield Aphrodite' (no.73; Red Room), but that might equally have been the 'Antique Head of Venus, excellent, Marble' which Brettingham the Younger recorded buying from Cavaceppi in 1753.[83] On 14 November Brettingham the Younger obtained the earl's 'subscription for moulds of statues and busts' (the busts are now in the White and Old Libraries; the latter not open to visitors). By 1758 Hamilton's bill amounted to nearly £300 and was slightly more in 1759. In 1760 the Earl laid out £315 for '11 Bustos' from the Wimbledon collection of Lyde Brown, and £160 on '4 busts' from Lord Dartmouth. This pattern of large annual payments to Hamilton (some £1,500 in 1760 and almost as much in 1762) continued until the earl's death. A typical cargo was the 'Eleven Cases containing Statues Busts and Tables of Marble' (and two pictures), which arrived in London from Leghorn (the port of Genoa) in 1761. '6 Marble Pedestals

The North Gallery: Central Corridor, looking east

value £83', Italian 'unbound books', Piranesi prints and '5 drawings on Paper/Value 207 gs' are also known to have been imported. Usually, the statues are not identified by subject, but on several occasions from 1761 to 1763 experts were sent to the London Custom House 'to set a value' on 'the Muse and Faun'; 'the Venus Apollo and Barberini Bustos'; 'the Young Nero and Bust of M. Aurelius'; the Sitting Consul and Philosopher (nos.15, 19); and 'the Juno and Ganimede' (nos.3, 1). This shows that several acquisitions were made from the famous collection in the Barberini Palace, and that the nine principal niches on the southern wall of the North Gallery were still being filled ten years after its construction. There was some further embellishment of the gallery in 1763, when 'moulding for Friezes, cornish etc' was supplied. The last shipment from Italy, which included a statue of Silenus, was made in 1765, two years after the death of the 2nd Earl, whose widow made the last payment to Gavin Hamilton.

The 1764 inventory reveals how the antique sculpture was displayed, and indicates that it was not all still in packing cases at the earl's sudden death (as tradition would have it). Far from being empty, the Petworth

The Red Room, looking north, with the recreation of the hang depicted by Turner in his gouache-watercolour view of *c.*1827

***Portrait Head of a Man* (detail), Roman, mid-3rd century AD.** Pentelic marble; top of head to point of chin, 28.5cm (no.38; North Gallery)

North Gallery was filled both with full-length statues in the niches and busts on brackets, apart from the two seated figures (nos.15, 19), which were originally placed on plinths within niches at one end. There were four other rooms with concentrations of statuary: the Marble Hall with its '2 Large Marble Statues' still in the niches, the 'Oak Room' (Little Dining Room) and two ante-rooms (which no longer exist) giving off the Great Staircase. One of these, on the first floor, had large marble busts in recesses (as in the North Gallery) and over the doors. The placing of statuary in such hallways was in conscious emulation of ancient Roman and post-Renaissance Italian practice. Petworth was also distinctive, both in 1764 and subsequently, for the use of classical statuary as decoration throughout the house. In 1784 a traveller noted that 'all the principal apartments are furnished with antique statues and busts, some of which are of first rate value'.[84] When the 2nd Earl placed an antique bust upon a marble-topped pier-table, for example, it was often flanked by blue-and-white porcelain, with larger jars beneath and on either side of the table. These arrangements (recorded in the 1764 inventory) were left untouched by the 3rd Earl, as shown in watercolours of the Petworth interiors by Turner and C.R. Leslie (Tate Britain and British Museum).

The antique statuary continued to excite comment long after the 2nd Earl's death, but a change in attitude can be detected even within the 18th century. Gavin Hamilton felt that the restoration of antique sculpture should not go too far: joins and cracks should not be unduly disguised and in his view it increased the sense of a statue's antiquity if it were left 'a little corroded and stained'. Cavaceppi stated that it is the role of the restorer to enlighten the antique fragment by judicious and discreet repairs and additions. In practice, both men condoned more radical restoration and re-working of antique fragments, but in the 1750s and 1760s most collectors shared their view that antique statuary should not be over-restored. Gradually, however, a smoother, more refined style of restoration (in accordance with Neo-classical sculpture) became more acceptable. It is interesting, therefore, that already by 1776 a visitor to Petworth described the marbles as 'lamentably patched',[85] an opinion reiterated by another visitor in 1784:

'Heroine, Petworth': Colossal Head **(detail), Greek, 4th century BC, made up later from two Greek fragments.** Pentelic marble, 90 cm high (no.27; North Gallery)

A singular circumstance attending them is, that a great many, when the late earl bought them, were complete invalids; some wanting heads, others hands, feet, noses, etc. These mutilations his lordship endeavoured to supply, by the application of new members, very ill suited either in complexion or elegance of finishing, to the Roman and Grecian trunks, so that in some respects this stately fabric gives us the idea of a large hospital, or receptacle, for wounded and disabled statues.[86]

Almost all the 2nd Earl's sculpture was retained by his son, the 3rd Earl, when he reached his majority, but one important statue, of *Artemis/Diana*, was alienated to his cousin, the Hon. George Grenville, later 1st Marquess of Buckingham, and acquired by the Earl of Lonsdale at the great sales from Stowe.[87]

The antique sculpture collection was expanded by the 3rd Earl, and although it was dismissed by Waagen in 1854 as 'of no high order, and chiefly restored works of the Roman time',[88] it contains two Greek masterpieces of the 4th century BC, the 'Leconfield Aphrodite', attributed to Praxiteles, and a contemporary Greek heroic female head of colossal size (nos.73, 27). Petworth is now of considerable rarity as the setting for the largest surviving 18th- and early 19th-century collection of antique sculpture in a British country house.

Until recently, the 2nd Earl's contribution to Petworth was not fully recognised: thus his role as a picture collector was unknown to C.H. Collins Baker, compiler of the 1920 picture catalogue. In view of his early death, and the remarkably prolific and prolonged collecting career of his son, the 3rd Earl, it is hardly surprising that his reputation as a Maecenas should have been eclipsed. His end was hastened by physical inertia and habitual over-indulgence. Horace Walpole recorded his demise at Egremont House on 21 August 1763:

Lord Egremont died suddenly, though everybody knew he would die suddenly; he used no exercise and could not be kept from eating, without which prodigious bleedings did not suffice: a day or two before he died, he said, 'Well, I have but three turtle dinners to come, and if I survive them I shall be immortal'. He was writing, as my Lady breakfasted, complained of a violent pain in his head, asked twice if he did not look very particularly, grew speechless, and expired that evening.[89]

5

The 3rd Earl of Egremont

George O'Brien Wyndham, 3rd Earl of Egremont (1751–1837) was a 12-year-old schoolboy at Westminster when his father died, aged 53, in 1763. The 3rd Earl was, however, destined to be long-lived, and his death almost 75 years later ended what has been called Petworth's golden age. There are numerous accounts of his hospitality, his wit, his dislike of ceremony, his great abilities combined with a preference for a private life, his kindness and generosity to the poor, to children and to the artists whom he encouraged. Egremont also shone as a benevolent landlord, an innovative farmer and as a breeder of horses, cattle and sheep. No other owner in the history of the turf has had five winners of both the Derby and the Oaks. In 1798 Egremont characteristically refused the presidency of the Board of Agriculture, but became increasingly famous for his experiments in crop rotation, in vegetable- and fruit-growing and in the development of planting tools such as the skim-coulter and the iron dibble. Hailed as 'one of the fathers of modern English agriculture',[90] he also put money into forward-looking schemes: his investment in the Chichester canal and the Brighton chain-pier is commemorated in paintings by Turner (Carved Room). He had the local population innoculated against smallpox, he erected or financed roads, waterways, hospitals, schools, almshouses, a gas works and Petworth Town Hall. 'It has been stated', wrote Mark Anthony Lower in 1865, 'that he spent in the course of sixty years in acts of charity and liberality, upwards of one million two hundred thousand pounds, or about £20,000 per annum.'[91] His annual income was estimated at £100,000 and he owned over 110,000 acres in the west of England, Cumberland, Yorkshire, Ireland and West Sussex.

To the impecunious painter Benjamin Robert Haydon, Lord Egremont was 'literally like the sun. The very flies at Petworth seem to know that there is room for their existence, that the windows are theirs'.[92] As well as the regular gatherings of family, friends and artists, at 'that princely seat of magnificent hospitality',[93] as Haydon put it,

[above]
***George O'Brien Wyndham, 3rd Earl of Egremont (1751–1837)*, by John Edward Carew (1785–1868), 1831.** Carrara marble, 76 x 59 x 33 cm (no.107; North Gallery)

[right]
***George O'Brien Wyndham, 3rd Earl of Egremont (1751–1837)*, by Thomas Phillips (1770–1845).** Oil on canvas, 139.7 x 110.5 cm (no.57; North Gallery)

there were tenants' and yeomanry dinners (in the Carved Room, North Gallery or Audit Room) and regal entertainments for the poor in the park. The greatest of these, when 6,000 were fed and waited on in medieval fashion by the local gentry, took place in May 1834. Witherington's painting of a summer fête in the park (no.27*; North Gallery) depicts Lord Egremont reigning 'in the dispensation of happiness'.[94] His *laissez-faire* benevolence surprised the traveller Louis Simond, used to the more exclusive attitudes of French landowners: 'He suffers the peasants of his village to play bowls and cricket on the lawn before the house; to scribble on the walls, and even on the glass of his windows.'[95] Egremont liked people to come and go as they pleased, and Petworth was consequently like a great inn where after 'conferring the greatest favours, he was out of the room before there was time to thank him'.[96]

The 3rd Earl was only 12 when he succeeded, too young to have been inculcated into his father's taste for art.[97] Nor does this taste appear to have manifested itself in him until his late 40s. He did buy a pair of Vernets of a *Seascape at Sunset* and a *Moonlit Landscape* (no longer identifiable) from the artist on a visit to Paris in 1773–4[98] (their purchase

Fête in Petworth Park, 1835 **by W.F. Witherington (1785–1865).** Oil on canvas, 84 x 120.5 cm (no.27*; North Gallery). **This depicts the 3rd Earl's second summer fête, laid on for 6,000 local people**

having possibly [there is no documentation] been inspired by the nearby group of Vernets at Uppark, especially as he was a close friend of Sir Harry Fetherstonhaugh, 2nd Bt, who had his own bedroom at Petworth); and it must have been he who acquired Stubbs's *Pomeranian Dog* and *'Trentham', with South up* (nos.40, 577**), each signed and dated 1773 (Petworth, Lord Egremont Collection),[99] but surely for the sake of the beasts rather than of their artist. There is also a tantalising, entirely unspecific, record of the purchase of sculpture and pictures at Lord Scarborough's sale at Christie's, via Brettingham the Younger in 1785.[100] But, after this one apparent emulation of his father, there was nothing further for 15 years or more – rather the reverse. As he withdrew from fashionable society, he gave up Egremont House in 1794, and blithely sent 170 paintings (and three plaster busts) to auction at Christie's, anonymously, as just the property of 'A Nobleman'.[101]

In his youth, the 3rd Earl's reputation had been as a man of fashion whose chief interest, according to the *Morning Herald* in 1782, was 'street riding'. He made two Grand Tours (between 1770 and 1774) visiting Dresden, Berlin, Prague and Vienna as well as Venice and Paris. In 1774 he ordered two services from the Royal Porcelain Manufactory at Sèvres, the first of which (10 July) is in the pattern *fleurs filets bleux* [flowers and blue ribbons], the second (17 October) is decorated with *rubans bleu céleste* [turquoise blue ribbons].[102] Pieces from both services remain at Petworth (Lord Egremont Collection, and NT).

'Voltaire and Rousseau were both alive …,' he remembered of London society at the time, 'and their art and their doctrines engrossed the attention of everybody … everything in fashionable life, dress, food, amusement, morals and manners all must be French … there was hardly a young lady of fashion who did not think it almost a stain on her reputation if she was not known to have cuckolded her husband.'[103] He imported a Parisian courtesan, Mlle Du Thé, who appeared 'all bediamonded' at the opera. His liaison with Lady Melbourne reputedly produced the 2nd Viscount Melbourne, the Prime Minister, and the latter's sister, Lady Palmerston (whose portrait by Lucas, no.352, hangs in the North Gallery). He was a close friend of Charles James Fox, the leader of the Whig opposition, and paid his gambling debts and those of Georgiana, Duchess of Devonshire.

In July 1780 he proposed to Lady Maria Waldegrave, whose uncle, Horace Walpole, wrote of Egremont: 'He is eight and twenty, is handsome, and has between twenty and thirty thousand a year. You may imagine he was not rejected by either mother or daughter'.[104] The engagement, however, was soon broken. To Walpole, Egremont was now 'a most worthless young fellow … weak and irresolute' who 'by new indiscretion, has drawn universal odium on himself'.[105] The impediment was probably Lord Egremont's philandering and, perhaps,

***The Last Judgement* by William Blake (1757–1827), 1808.** Pen and ink, pencil and watercolour on paper, 50.3 x 40 cm (no.454; North Gallery).

the realisation that he valued his freedom more than a respectable alliance. In about 1784 the 15-year-old Elizabeth Iliffe, or Ilive, became his principal mistress and the unofficial chatelaine of Petworth. She was the daughter of a master at Westminster School, and bore Egremont six children before their secret marriage in 1801. According to the diarist Joseph Farington, Mrs Wyndham (as she was known before her marriage) 'took great delight in painting', both as an artist and as a patron.[106] In 1798 he noted that she planned to see the great Orléans collection of pictures then on exhibition in London following its purchase by a syndicate of English noblemen. She commissioned two paintings by William Blake (nos.427, 454; North Gallery) and was also an amateur scientist who set up a private laboratory at Petworth.

Despite their happiness and shared artistic interests, the 3rd Earl pursued other amours (his continued infidelities provoked a separation), and even hung their portraits at Petworth, as the famous letter writer Thomas Creevey noted with amusement in 1828, writing of 'my Lord's Seraglio'. Egremont's reputation as a womaniser convinced one Society lady that:

> he had forty-three children who all live in the house with him and their respective Mothers; that the latter are usually kept in the background, but that when any quarrels arise, which few days pass without, each Mother takes part with her Progeny, bursts into the drawing room, fight with each other, Ld. E. and his Children, and I believe the Company, and make scenes worthy of Billingsgate or a Mad House.[107]

Certainly, as Creevey put it, 'old Egremont had a very numerous stud' (a *double-entendre* by reference to his racing stable),[108] and he was very fond of children 'who always came away [from his dressing room] with a sugar-plum, or some other little present'. To Lady Holland, who did not like 'to miss any opportunity of enjoying his society', Lord Egremont was a 'patriarch' whose house was 'a strange medley … artists and their wives and large numbers of their children'.[109] Most of the colourful accounts of staying at Petworth as a guest of the 3rd Earl date from towards the end of his life, when visiting artists were entranced by their kind reception. In 1798 arrangements had been more formal. According to Farington, when there was no company, the artists dined with Lord Egremont and Mrs Wyndham, but 'when company was expected they dined with Mrs Wyndham only'.[110] Thomas Daniell, the painter of Indian landscapes, 'found Egremont good natured, but with much of the peer in him, the effect of a habit of authority'. Haydon, who had recently languished in a debtors' prison and whose sole commission from Lord Egremont was the rather unsatisfactory *Alexander the Great taming Bucephalus* (no.660; North Gallery) left perhaps the most telling description of Petworth in the 3rd Earl's day (in 1826):

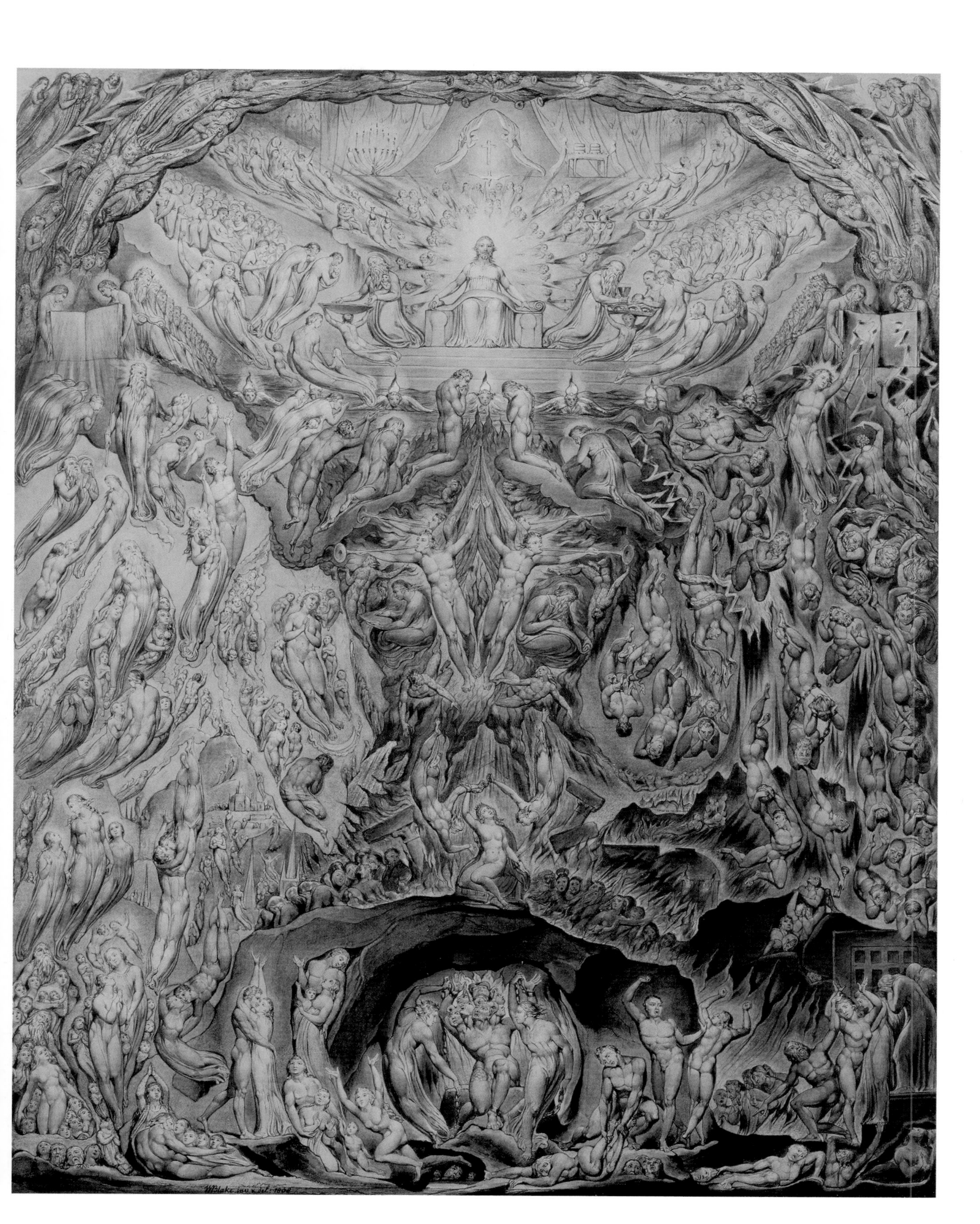

***Mrs Robinson (1803)* by William Owen (1769–1825), exhibited at the Royal Academy in 1803.**
Oil on canvas, 200 x 175 cm
(no.13; North Gallery)

He has placed me in one of the most magnificent bedrooms I ever saw, [hung with ancestral portraits on green damask], and a beautiful view of the park from the high windows.... At breakfast, after the guests have all breakfasted, in walks Lord Egremont; first comes a grandchild, whom he sends away happy. Outside the window ... a dozen black Spaniels, who are let in, and to them he distributes cakes and comfits, giving all equal shares. After chatting with one guest, and proposing some scheme of pleasure to others, his leathern gaiters are buttoned on, and away he walks, leaving everybody to take care of themselves, with all that opulence and generosity can place at their disposal entirely within their reach. At dinner he meets everybody and then are recounted the feats of the day. All principal dishes he helps, never minding the trouble of carving; he eats heartily and helps liberally. There is plenty, but not absurd profusion; good wines, but not extravagant waste. Everything solid, liberal, rich and English. [I] sketched and studied all day [and dined] with the finest Vandyke in the world.[111]

Haydon concluded that Egremont was 'of the old school who considered a great artist fit society for any man, however high his rank, and at his table ... all were as equals'.[112] Sophisticated guests were sometimes more critical. In 1823 the Hon. Edward Fox noted: 'The want of comforts, of regularity, and still more the total absence of clean linens, made it, splendid and beautiful as it is, far from being agreeable. Society too seems as little attended to as anything else. People of all descriptions, without any connections or acquaintance with each other, are gathered together and huddled up at the dinner table'.[113] To Charles Greville, Lord Egremont 'lives with an abundant though not very refined hospitality. The house wants modern comforts, and the servants are rude and uncouth; but everything is good, and it all bears an air of solid and aristocratic grandeur.'[114] In 1773 the Petworth servants' new liveries ('the postilions have white jackets trimmed with muslin, and clean ones every two days')[115] had struck Horace Walpole as the height of fashionable extravagance. By 1826 'the liveries were extremely plain' (as was Egremont's own dress), but 'there were more [servants] in that house, of both sexes and in all departments than in any House in England'.[116] They kept their master's early hours. Creevey, asking for a glass of wine at 10.30pm, was told by the footman that 'the Butler was gone to bed' but he noted that 'in the morning they are at their posts with the lark'.[117]

***Sleeping Venus and Cupid* by John Hoppner (*c.*1758–1810).** Oil on canvas, 132 x 168 cm (no.24; North Gallery)

The Square Dining Room looking south. Re-creation of the picture hang and the furniture arrangement depicted in Turner's view opposite

[right]
***The South Wall of the Square Dining Room*, by J.M.W. Turner (1775–1851), 1827.** Watercolour and gouache on blue paper, 13.8 x 18.8 cm (Tate)

The 3rd Earl made his first alterations at Petworth in 1774, when he commissioned Matthew Brettingham the Younger to convert the King of Spain's Bedchamber into the White Library. The bookshelves are still surmounted by plaster busts after the antique, presumably from the moulds acquired by Brettingham when he was acting as the 2nd Earl's agent in Rome. Around 1777–8 the 3rd Earl modified the west front by taking down the Proud Duke's dome and statues. He also lowered the ground-floor windows to make it easier for his guests to step into the park. After selling Egremont House in 1794, he bought a smaller house in Grosvenor Place, but his mind was clearly turning to Petworth, where he was resuming his building activities with the enlargement of the Carved Room as a museum of the carvings by Gibbons and Selden and the creation of the Square Dining and Somerset rooms. In the 3rd Earl's time all the principal rooms were painted white or red, and the curtains the length of the west front were of crimson or scarlet silk or moreen. The gilt pier-glasses and tables flanked by 17th-century blue-and-white porcelain jars remained much as his father had arranged them, and sculpture continued to be deployed throughout the apartments. Whereas his father had kept all his Old Masters in London, the mixture of paintings at Petworth now became more catholic, as his father's remaining pictures and the inherited Percy collections were expanded by the 3rd Earl's purchases and commissions. The estate yard accounts are replete with references to the continuous wanderings of this 'infinity of pictures [and] statues'.[118] From 1791 men were continually 'taking down and putting up pictures in the house', making frames, providing stretchers and easels and constructing pedestals and plinths for statues. Pictures were also transported in packing cases to and fro between Petworth and London, often for exhibition at the British Institution or the Royal Academy. At Egremont's death, there were (and remain) more than 600 pictures in the collection, and his purchases of antique sculpture and his sculptural patronage prompted the extension of the North Gallery between 1824 and 1827.

In 1827 Thomas Creevey was amazed by 'the *immensity* of pictures on the ground floor of the house, and, as I was informed, all the rooms above are full of them. Then they are all mixed up together, good and bad, and he [the 3rd Earl] is perpetually changing their places'.[119] Turner's sketches of about the same date show that, despite the miscellany, the pictures were usually arranged symmetrically in well-balanced tiers. Creevey had been 'rather fidgetty in the morning to be about the house after the pictures', and had just started a tour before breakfast when 'old Egremont came *slouching* by':

> 'Pray, Lord Egremont, what is that curious picture....?' 'Ah!', says he, 'it is a devilish clever picture, is it not. Let's go look at it;' and so we did.... He slouched along the rooms with his hat on and his hands in his breeches pockets, making occasional observations upon the pictures and statues, which were always agreeable and instructive, but so rambling and desultory, and walking on all the time, that it was quite provoking to pass so rapidly over such valuable materials.[120]

As a patron, Egremont is most famous for fostering 'rising genius'[121] in his friendship with J.M.W. Turner, by whom there are no fewer than 20 paintings at Petworth. He bought his first Turner, *Ships Bearing up for Anchorage*, also known as the 'Egremont Seapiece' (no.33; North Gallery), around 1802. Furthermore, Egremont's name appears in an entry for 1783 in Sir Joshua Reynolds's ledgers; in 1785 he bought prints by Hogarth and in 1795 commissioned a portrait of Mrs Wyndham and her children from George Romney (no.381; Lord Egremont Collection),

who had long had the 'ambition to place some work of his pencil in the princely mansion of Petworth'.[122] Subject pictures by James Barry, Sir Francis Bourgeois, Henry Fuseli and John Opie may also have been acquired early in his collecting career. He was also one of only two aristocratic purchasers at the sale of Alderman Boydell's Shakespeare Gallery in 1805. However, it was from the late 1790s that he flourished as a patron and collector of British art. His personal papers were apparently destroyed after his death, and his collecting activities have to be pieced together from a variety of other sources.

Petworth had already become a veritable academy by 1798, when the gem-engraver Nathaniel Marchant 'saw in the great Hall there, several pictures of Vandyke standing, and Collins, the Miniature painter, Phillips, the Portrait painter – and a Clergyman from Cambridge copying them – this was liberally allowed them to do by Lord Egremont'. The previous year, Romney had suggested that Thomas Hayley (a pupil of Flaxman) should 'pursue his professional studies in the gallery of his noble friend at Petworth',[123] where, according to Haydon, he produced 'a small copy in clay' of a seated antique statue, presumably one of the two sedentary figures (nos.15, 19), which in those days faced each other at either end of the then unextended North Gallery. Constable remembered of a visit to Petworth in 1834 that 'the Gainsborough [probably no.106; North Gallery] was down when I was there. I placed it as it suited me, and I cannot think of it now without tears in my eyes.'[124] The painter C.R. Leslie was allowed to hang 'a gem' by Bassano in his bedroom.[125] There are three sketches by Turner of artists at work in the Old Library. This huge room above the Chapel, with an immense east window, was ideal for the purpose, and was hung rather haphazardly with numerous pictures. In 1835 there

[left]
***The Carved Room*, by Charles Robert Leslie (1794–1859), *c.*1828.**
Oil on wood, 35.2 x 30 cm (Tate)

[below]
The Carved Room showing the west and north walls, with an open door looking to the Red Room, recreating the view painted by C.R. Leslie opposite

were 55 – the usual Petworth mix of Old Masters and contemporary paintings including works by Blake and Fuseli, and portraits by Hoppner and Beechey, who is probably depicted by Turner painting one of them here. When Turner had locked himself into his studio, only Lord Egremont was allowed to enter, but on one famous occasion Turner was fooled by his friend Sir Francis Chantrey's imitation of the earl's distinctive tread on the staircase and knock on the door. Turner, Beechey, Chantrey, Phillips and Leslie were of the inner circle of Lord Egremont's artistic friends and during their long stays 'were always made to feel quite at home'. Chantrey and Phillips are known to have given advice on Egremont's 'projects in adorning his house', and it is likely that Turner's opinion was also sought.

The 3rd Earl's patronage of Turner fell into two parts.[126] At first – from the acquisition of *Ships Bearing up for Anchorage* that was exhibited, but not necessarily immediately acquired by the 3rd Earl, at the Royal Academy in 1802, to his purchases of *Hulks on the Tamar* (no.656; North Gallery) and *Teignmouth* (no.658; North Gallery), both of 1812 – the 3rd Earl was simply a buyer of Turner's oils. At this stage, it appears that he had never bought a watercolour, by Turner or anyone else, save Blake – and it was Lady Egremont who bought Blake's watercolour *The Last Judgement* in 1808 (no.454; North Gallery). The earl apparently made his acquisitions from the annual exhibitions Turner had of his own work in his Harley Street house, in the gallery the artist had built for the purpose in 1804. In 1809 Egremont also commissioned two views of his own seats: *Cockermouth Castle* (no.653; North Gallery) and *Petworth: Dewy Morning* (no.636; White Library).

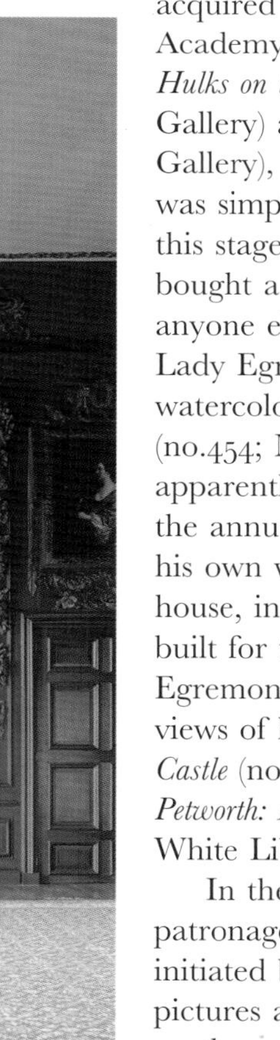

In the second phase of Egremont's patronage of Turner, seemingly initiated by the 3rd Earl's buying pictures at Lord de Tabley's posthumous auction at Christie's in July 1827, including Turner's *Tabley, Calm Morning* (no.8), the artist became a regular guest at Petworth, where one of the rooms (not, as in the misleading tradition, the Old Library, but near it)[127] was allocated to him as a studio. A kind of competitive camaraderie seems to have grown up between host and guest. Both had irregular liaisons, and stood outside the conventional norms of their respective social spheres. Petworth was a kind of Liberty Hall, where, as Creevey sardonically noted, 'artists are always allowed to do what they liked', and the 3rd Earl, as Beechey said of him, had 'more "put-up-ability" than almost any man'.[128] Benjamin Robert Haydon, despite the patronage that Lord Egremont very deliberately gave him, was never invited back to stay a second time after the six days that he spent there in 1826, doubtless because of obsequiousness that was anathema to the earl.[129] Much more his style was arguing with Turner over whether certain vegetables would float in salt water, testing the point with him, and winning.[130] Turner then impudently and unrepentantly showed those same vegetables bobbing on the water of his *The Chain Pier, Brighton* (no.140; Carved Room). Yet even the easy-going 3rd Earl seems to have objected to the lack of decorum of being painted by Turner walking out from the house to the lake, followed by a motley crew of dogs, in a picture that would have been at eye level with guests sitting down to eat in the Carved Room. This was the first version (Tate) of *Petworth Park* or *The Lake, Petworth: Sunset, Fighting Bucks* (no.132; Carved Room).[131]

By 1828 three landscapes were already fixed in the Carved Room. It is probable that by 1830 all four were installed – replaced *in situ* in 2002, when the Carved Room was restored. These were given carved wooden frames in Gibbons-esque style by Jonathan Ritson, a carver who was employed for over 18 years to provide additional carvings to complement the originals by Gibbons. Two of Turner's Carved Room

***Petworth Park* or *The Lake, Petworth: Sunset, Fighting Bucks*, by J.M.W. Turner (1775–1851), *c*.1829.** Oil on canvas, 62 x 146 cm (no.132; Carved Room) (Tate)

paintings are depictions of Petworth park, which also inspired numerous sketches in gouache and watercolour. Over 120 sheets of light blue paper (Tate) reveal Turner's private reactions to Petworth's interiors and landscape. Despite Ruskin's classification of them as 'Rubbish', 'Inferior', and 'Worse', they are among Turner's most beautiful and immediate works. They range from the sketchiest shorthand note of a single figure or of the effect of changing light in the park to more detailed studies of views and interiors. Since 1991 the more finished sketches – those of the Square Dining Room, North Gallery and Red Room in particular – have informed the re-creation of picture hangs and schemes of decoration admired by Turner.

In 1834 Turner's great contemporary, John Constable, was also a guest of Lord Egremont, who 'ordered one of his carriages to be ready every day, to enable Constable to see as much of the neighbourhood as possible'. According to his friend and fellow guest, C.R. Leslie, Constable 'filled a large book with sketches in pencil and watercolours, some of which he finished very highly.... He rose early, and had often made some beautiful sketch in the park before breakfast.... His dressing table was covered with flowers, feathers of birds, and pieces of bark with lichens adhering to them which he had brought home for the sake of their beautiful tints'.[132] Constable declared: 'Claude nor Ruysdael could not do a thousandth part of what nature here represents',[133] but his failure to receive a commission from Lord Egremont led him, incorrectly, to assume that 'landscape affords him no interest whatever'.[134]

'On matters of art', wrote C.R. Leslie, 'Lord Egremont thought for himself; and his remarks were worth remembering. He said to me: "I look upon Raphael and Hogarth as the two greatest painters that ever lived".'[135] His tastes were catholic and he bought Old Masters and antique sculpture as well as commissioning portraits, landscapes and historical works. As a patron, the 3rd Earl seems to have had two prime motivations. One was simply to give his patronage to British artists who might not have flourished without it – which would very probably have been the case with Clint and Derby, if not with Phillips (who, after all, among other things, painted a celebrated portrait of Byron). The other was to encourage artists to tackle ideal subjects, rather than the literalness of portraiture. This he did in sculpture, successfully with Flaxman and Carew, but unsuccessfully with Chantrey; and in painting, successfully with Leslie, but unsuccessfully with Phillips. He never sat to any of the fashionable portrait painters of his day and told Leslie: 'I wish to keep you employed on such [historical and literary] subjects instead of portraits'.[136] The North Gallery is filled with pictures and sculpture in tune with Egremont's literary tastes. Works inspired by Chaucer, Spenser, Shakespeare, Milton, Swift, Thomson, Prior, Beattie,

Horace and Cervantes by a succession of British artists, including Reynolds, Turner, Fuseli, Opie, Clint, Northcote, Thomson, Leslie, Blake, Flaxman, Rossi and Westmacott, are placed alongside biblical, mythological and historical subjects by many of those painters and sculptors as well as Carew, Nollekens, Haydon and Phillips. Following the 1991–3 restoration, the gallery also contains Old Masters, portraits and landscapes, as it did in 1835, when at Petworth Turner's landscapes were confined to the North Gallery and the Carved Room.[137]

If the 3rd Earl's patronage of historical painting was enlightened at a time when, in Haydon's words, 'practical England feels no natural love of Art except of the imitative kind',[138] his sculptural commissions were quite exceptional. Most contemporary patrons of sculpture favoured the Italians, and Canova in particular. In 1819, during an *incognito* visit to Chantrey's studio, Lord Egremont asked him whether he had ever departed from portraiture by modelling 'an ideal subject, or anything from poetry'. Chantrey replied: 'Our patrons do not give commissions for such subjects, at least not to English artists; the only sculptor among us who has been employed on anything of the kind is Flaxman, who has a commission from Lord Egremont.'[139] The 6th Duke of Devonshire, whose collection, still at Chatsworth, consisted almost entirely of works by Canova and his followers, would subsequently regret his failure to commission a statue from Flaxman, but by then the sculptor was dead. Lord Egremont owned two, including a masterpiece, *St Michael overcoming Satan* (1819–26, the subject taken from Milton's *Paradise Lost*), around which the North or Square Bay of the North Gallery was built in 1826–7. Apart from St Michael's spear, it was carved from a single block of marble at a cost of £3,500, and according to the 3rd Earl's inscription on the base, 'Flaxman's achievement was hardly surpassed by the most celebrated productions of ancient times, and certainly by none of his own.'

***The Carved Room*, c.1865, by Hon. Mrs Percy (Madeline) Wyndham.**
Gouache and watercolour on paper, 40.4 x 45.5 cm. (no.705; Carved Room; Lord Egremont Collection)

The principal (east) wall of Carved Room, looking north

Two other important compositions suggested by poetry are *Celadon and Amelia* (*c.*1821; no.105; South Corridor, North Gallery) by J.C.F. Rossi, the dramatic subject taken from Thomson's *Seasons* and, inspired by Horace's *Ode to Calliope, The Dream of Horace*, a bas-relief (exhibited and 'just completed' in 1823; no.111) by Sir Richard Westmacott, who personally installed it in the wall at the west end of the North Gallery. Westmacott, nicknamed 'Westmacotteles' by Egremont because of his airs and his addiction to all things Greek, was a regular visitor to Petworth in the 1820s, and probably advised his host on matters of display, given his responsibility for the presentation of sculpture at the British Museum.

The influence of Canova is not absent from the North Gallery, and is evident in Westmacott's *Nymph and Cupid* (exhibited 1827; no.98), which was carved from a single block of marble, and perhaps also in Rossi's *British Pugilist* (exhibited 1828; no.99), which is reminiscent of Canova's *Pugilists* in the Vatican. Rossi's plea for more money in 1826, while working on this statue, for once failed to arouse Lord Egremont's sympathy: 'Lord Egremont, in answer to Rossi's letter, told him that he had nothing to do with his marble, that [he] must finish his statue, and send it home, that in mode of application he forgot his, Lord E's, Rank, as well as his own.... Rossi, I suppose, applied in the style of a butcher', concluded B.R. Haydon with satisfaction (Rossi had been his landlord

[left]
***The North Gallery from the North Bay: Owen's Portrait of Mrs Robinson Hanging to the Left of Flaxman's 'St Michael Overcoming Satan'*, by J.M.W. Turner (1775–1851), *c.*1827.**
Gouache and watercolour on paper, 13.8 x 18.9 cm. (Tate)

[below]
***An Artist Seated before Sir William Beechey's Portrait 'Mrs Hasler as Flora'*, by J.M.W. Turner (1775–1851), *c.*1827.**
Gouache and watercolour on paper, 14 x 19.3 cm. (Tate)

and treated him badly over rent arrears).[140] Other sculptors commissioned by the 3rd Earl included George Garrard (portrait busts and small models of prize cattle) and Joseph Nollekens (a portrait bust of Lord Egremont dated 1815). That the earl also bought Nollekens's plaster *Seated Venus* at his posthumous studio sale in 1823, and commissioned a marble copy of it by Rossi's assistant, Richard Williams, indicates his regard for this distinguished sculptor of a previous generation. It also suggests the conscious compilation of a representative collection of contemporary British sculpture.

Egremont encouraged Sir Francis Chantrey to turn away from his habitual portraits to produce an ideal work: 'a capital figure of Satan, with something of his original brightness'. This project 'was destined to tease the sculptor, more or less, as long as he lived. He knew that expectation had been raised, and he felt at once the difficulties of the task, and the peril – or rather the certainty of failure', wrote Chantrey's biographer in 1851.[141] A young Irish sculptor, John Edward Carew, had no such qualms, and having come to Lord Egremont's notice in 1813, was almost exclusively employed by him from about 1820. A former assistant of Westmacott, he was praised by Haydon in 1826 as 'perhaps the best cutter of marble in England .... as rapid as lightening [*sic*] with his chisel, but idle in thought, preferring the chat of a gossiping Coffee House to the glory of fame'.[142] His 'light spirits', 'gay mind' and his Irish charm certainly appealed to Lord Egremont, who found that Carew's 'Genius and Conception' was in tune with his own taste for 'colossal works of heroic size'.[143] Egremont not only gave him 'subjects to illustrate', but closely followed their progress, cancelling more than one commission when well advanced. Carew was later to criticise what he called his patron's 'capricious and sudden' changes of heart. Until 1831, Carew remained in London, producing there an *Adonis* (1823–5/6; no.100) and the colossal group of *Venus, Vulcan and Cupid* (*c.*1827/8–31; no.115), for which he received £4,000 (£500 more than Flaxman for his slightly smaller *St Michael*). These were placed in the North Gallery, completed in 1827, which Egremont intended to further alter under Carew's direction. Due to a severe illness, however, Lord Egremont put a stop to these plans.

From 1832 to 1837, Carew lived near Petworth and was also provided with a studio at Brighton, where Egremont had a house. In the final year of his life, the 3rd Earl, ever eager to be building, was constructing 'a new dining room for the tenants' [the present tea-room]. 'At the time,' remembered Carew, 'I was working on a large group of Prometheus; and after moving it into this new hall, Lord Egremont called it the "Promethean Hall".'[144] This was the heroic group (no.116) now in the North Gallery, from which the 3rd Earl had removed Carew's *Venus, Vulcan and Cupid* to place it at the opposite end of the Promethean Gallery. This second gallery, doubling as a tenants' hall and hung with cattle pictures in recognition of the farmers who were given dinner there, was clearly intended as a museum of Carew's sculpture, but the enterprise was curtailed by the 3rd Earl's death. The Square Bay of the North Gallery now contains almost all of Carew's commissioned sculpture.[145]

The Old Library: a recreation of the arrangement depicted in Turner's view opposite

Carew's insolvency led him to sue Lord Egremont's executors for the astonishing

Arethusa **(detail), by John Edward Carew (1785–1868), 1824.** Marble, 137 cm high (no.103; North Gallery)

sum of £50,000, despite the lavish payments that he had received during Lord Egremont's lifetime. The published proceedings of the ensuing court cases (1841–2), in which Westmacott and Chantrey appeared as expert witnesses, are an important document not only as an illustration of Carew's relationship with his patron but for its rarity as a record of sculptural practice in early 19th-century England.[146] Because Carew lost the cases against the 3rd Earl's executors, in which he claimed what he maintained was owing to him, it has always been taken for granted that he was in the wrong – and was in fact indebted to the 3rd Earl, rather than vice versa. A careful reading of the proceedings of the two court cases, however, reveals that his claims were entirely justified. The 3rd Earl had encouraged him to give up a very profitable practice in London, where he had been using his exceptional skills as a carver to work lucratively, above all, for Westmacott.[147] He had then come down first to Brighton, and then to Petworth, to work almost exclusively for the 3rd Earl, or on commissions that he put the sculptor forward for, and also as a virtual factotum. He was indeed paid for his finished works, but there were a number of full-size plasters – notably, in pursuit of the 3rd Earl's obsession, a figure of *Satan* – that failed to meet with his patron's satisfaction, which he was ordered to destroy. Though, as the result of the second case, Carew was declared a bankrupt, he evidently did not forfeit public sympathy. There was a burst of forbidden applause in court after his counsel's closing peroration on his behalf, and he continued to receive important commissions, including for the relief of *The Death of Nelson* (1849) on the base of Nelson's Column. And although his exhibits at the Royal Academy never won him even Associate status there, so that he signed the *Monument to the Percy Family* (1837) in Petworth church: *Proh Pudor Academiae non Academicus*

('To the shame of the Academy not an Academician'), they awarded him a donation shortly before his death in reduced circumstances as he had not been able to work for a number of years. The seated figure of the monument to the 3rd Earl of Egremont (1840) in the church at Petworth was executed instead by the ubiquitous E.H. Baily (1788–1867).

To Carew, and to the other artists whom he befriended, Lord Egremont was indeed a 'Sussex Maecenas'. His gift of £1,000 to Sir William Beechey, who 'had a large family', and his encouragement of 'rising genius' through commissions and influential support were described by Lady Holland as 'acts of kindness that he is doing perpetually'.[148] His patronage was exceptional for its encouragement of British artists, and his commissions for heroic sculpture were virtually unique. He took a close interest in the subject-matter of a picture or statue, arranging for Haydon to make equestrian studies in the Guards' Riding School, and in the last months of his life rummaging in the attic to find a prop for one of Leslie's paintings. His open-handed hospitality gave Petworth the character of a luxurious academy, where Turner and Constable could be equally inspired by the Proud Duke's 'grand and solemn' Claude, or by the natural beauty of the park. To Leslie, Lord Egremont was 'the most munificent, and at the same time the least ostentatious nobleman in England'.[149] He disliked 'ribbons and higher titles', and his refusal of the Garter was typical. His multifarious activities encompassed the arts and sciences. To Creevey, he was 'as extraordinary a person, perhaps as any in England; certainly the most so of his own caste or order'. On hearing of his death, Charles Greville concluded that it would 'be more felt within the sphere of his influence ... than any individual's ever was'.[150] Leslie described his funeral in Petworth parish church in November 1837:

> All the shops in the town were closed, and business entirely suspended. Indeed all the inhabitants were present, either following the procession, or lining the way as it passed. There was not a single carriage. All the mourners followed the coffin on foot, and the line was continued to a great length. The many artists who had enjoyed his patronage, Turner, Phillips, Carew, Clint, and myself, were present.[151]

***The Dream of Horace* (detail), by Sir Richard Westmacott (1775–1856), 1823;** 140 x 184 cm (no.11; North Gallery)

6

19th- and 20th-century Petworth

The Square Dining Room, looking north-east

The 3rd Earl's eldest son, George (1787–1869), inherited his father's possessions but could not inherit his titles due to his illegitimacy. The earldom (and the Orchard Wyndham and Devon estates) devolved upon the 3rd Earl's nephew and became extinct on his (the 4th Earl's) death in 1845. George Wyndham was known as Colonel Wyndham after 1830, when he was appointed Colonel of the 24th Foot, and in 1859 he was created Lord Leconfield, the name of a Percy fortress and estate in Yorkshire which had come into the family in the 14th century. Like his father, he was a keen sportsman, and he and his younger brother, Henry, both kept packs of hounds – 'the only instance in the sporting world of two brothers each keeping a pack of foxhounds', declared the legendary hunting commentator, 'Nimrod', in 1824.[152] After their father's death, the brothers fell out over the demarcation of their hunting countries, which led to a long and bitter feud. According to Leconfield's great-grandson, John Wyndham:

> George was shy, taciturn and solitary – traits which he had inherited from his father without his father's sensibility. Perhaps their bastardy had given him and Henry chips on their shoulders. Anyway, they both had vile tempers. Neither brother was an intelligent or cultivated man. George's affections were strong though not diffuse: they embraced his wife, his children and the chase.[153]

Henry had distinguished himself at the Battle of Vittoria in 1813, where he captured the fleeing King Joseph Bonaparte's carriage, which was filled with over 200 rolled-up Old Masters looted from Spanish collections (many now at Apsley House, London). His presence also at Waterloo explains his father's choice of subjects for George Jones's battle pictures in the Beauty Room, the Petworth shrine to British military mastery over the French.

The 1st Lord Leconfield's management of Petworth was exemplary and conservative. Charles Barry submitted an estimate 'for proposed alterations and additions at Petworth House', which included a 'New

approach and Entrance on the East Side' in 1839, but they were not executed. Lord Leconfield completed his father's scheme for the Carved Room, continuing to employ Jonathan Ritson until 1846. He had the paintings numbered, the hang of pictures throughout the house recorded, and a basic printed catalogue was published in 1856. In 1854 he had pictures varnished and in 1856 had them cleaned by H.R. Bolton, who had drawn up illustrated lists in 1847. Pictures continued to be loaned to the British Institution exhibitions, and G.F. Waagen, the peripatetic German expert who described the collection in 1854 as 'in extent and value, one of the finest in England', was granted a 'very polite reception'.[154]

The house was extensively repaired during Lord Leconfield's time, the 3rd Earl's clerk of works, Mr Upton, remaining in post, but there were few alterations until Salvin's, immediately after Lord Leconfield's death in 1869. His daughter-in-law, Constance, wife of Henry, 2nd Lord Leconfield, who first came to Petworth in 1867 after their honeymoon at Uppark, recorded her reminiscences of the house in *Random Papers*, and it is evident that remarkably little had changed since the 3rd Earl's death in 1837. Lord Leconfield she described as 'a shy and affectionate man of 80 who still followed his hounds in a brougham' and who 'had what is called the "Wyndham temper", and he used very forcible language at times'.[155] According to his third son, Percy, he had a deep love and understanding of the country and of agriculture, 'his keen common sense going to the root of everything'. His adored wife, Mary, was 'deeply religious, of the pronounced Evangelical type' and was 'also very strict as to conventions, and what she considered due to her position as mistress of Petworth. No familiar intercourse was allowed with the town, the children and servants were forbidden to go into it, and she herself never entered it except in a carriage'.[156] The carriage and horses accompanied her on the train to London and as Lady Leconfield would not 'travel with strangers … the upper servants at Petworth always travelled first class and filled the vacant seats in her compartment'. The Petworth housekeeper was Mrs Smith,

The north wall of the Beauty Room: above are Dahl's portraits (originally full-length) of Queen Anne's court ladies; below Phillips's portrait (1802) of Napoleon between George Jones's depictions of the battles of Vittoria (1813) and Waterloo (1815). On the table stands Chantrey's bust (1828) of the Duke of Wellington

***The Marble Hall*, by Hon. Mrs Percy (Madeline) Wyndham, *c.*1865.**
Gouache and watercolour on paper, 29.8 x 49.2 cm (no.705; Marble Hall; Lord Egremont Collection)

who served the family for over 30 years, and who, after Lady Leconfield's death in 1863, ensured that her late mistress's rules were observed:

> No maid was allowed to go into the town, their dress was most severely regulated, no hat could be allowed in church on Sundays … attendance at church was strictly enforced, and the whole household sat in the gallery in pairs rising in tiers behind the family seats. When some experts came down to view the pictures, and expressed opinions as to their genuineness: 'How should they know more than the late Lady Leconfield?' said Mrs Smith, and to her that settled the matter.[157]

After his wife's death, Lord Leconfield lived a retired life, and 'never again asked a stranger into Petworth House'.[158] His occupation of the Marble Hall as a cluttered and carpeted study is recorded in a view painted about 1865 by his daughter-in-law, Madeline, wife of his favourite son, Percy (no.705; Marble Hall). The Percy Wyndhams used to spend most of the winter at Petworth with their three children, their nurse and nurserymaid.

The 1st Lord Leconfield's death in 1869 ushered in a decade of considerable changes to Petworth. The fashionable architect Anthony Salvin was immediately summoned by Henry, 2nd Lord Leconfield, and was commissioned to undertake major alterations at the south end of the house (which had always been the family's domestic quarters). The carriage drive from the west was now diverted from the Marble Hall, and led via iron gates (copies of Tijou's gates at Hampton Court) to a new main entrance on the east or town side. Salvin screened off the south end from the servants' block and courtyard (the Fountain Court), from which the 3rd Earl's fountain was removed to enliven the private garden. The roofed real tennis court enclosing the north end of the old Fountain Court was demolished (it was rebuilt in its present position next to the estate yard) and the view to the Pleasure Ground opened up. New stables were built, creating an enlarged stable courtyard while preserving the 18th-century stable range, and the Church Lodge (the town entrance) was erected alongside. The most radical alteration to the

principal rooms was the remodelling of the 3rd Earl's enlarged Carved Room. Here Salvin's builders, Charles Smith of 44 Upper Baker Street, London, removed the 3rd Earl's grey-white paint from panelling and doors, so that Gibbons's and Selden's carvings were seen, as originally, upon a darker oak background. Most of Ritson's carvings were removed, as were the landscapes by Turner, and the dado and fireplaces were altered. Morris & Co. provided green silk damask in 'Larkspur' pattern for sections of the panelling and for new curtains and pelmets. The 2nd Lord Leconfield also removed paint from 17th-century carvings and doors in the 'Vandyke Room' (the Little Dining Room), and repainted several other rooms, including the Marble Hall, North Gallery and Square Dining Room. Percy and Madeline Wyndham were both in the vanguard of the Arts and Crafts movement, commissioning Philip Webb in 1881 to build Clouds, near Salisbury, Wiltshire, the epitome of an Arts and Crafts country house.[159] This must explain the employment of the William Morris firm by the 2nd and 3rd Lords Leconfield to provide wallpapers, damask wall-coverings, upholstery, curtains, carpets and lamps for Petworth, including some extremely rare printed velvets. Unfortunately, the date of this commission or commissions is not known, although it is certain that the 2nd Lord Leconfield hung the Morris silk in the Carved Room between 1869 and 1901, and probably in the 1870s.

Constance Leconfield (who noted that 'Morris cretonnes' became fashionable in the 1870s) and her sister-in-law Madeline were close friends, who both insisted that their husbands should make up an earlier

[left]
The Carved Room as it was before the restoration (completed 2002) of the 3rd Earl's scheme and the re-fixing of the Turner landscapes into the lower section of the panelling

quarrel which blew up 'over the port and their inheritance'. The younger brother, Percy, had been treated extremely generously in his father's will, which allowed him to commission the building of Clouds. The truce was ratified by an invitation to Clouds, where Lord Leconfield 'was bitten in the hall by Percy's dog'; and spent the night 'worrying whether he was going to get hydrophobia'. This annoyed Constance Leconfield's elder brother, Lord Rosebery, then Prime Minister, 'who resented other people in his circle being as neurotic as he was'.[160]

The 2nd Lord Leconfield's building activities extended to London where he gave up the 3rd Earl's house in Grosvenor Place and built Leconfield House in Chesterfield Gardens, Mayfair. Again, Salvin was his architect, although the building was completed after 1879 by George Aitchison, who had earlier altered the Percy Wyndhams' Berkeley Square house. Lord Leconfield 'had barrels of drinking-water sent up from Petworth. He always said that he not going to risk his children catching typhoid fever from drinking the London water'. The 'mad business' of carting water from Petworth to London ended with the death on 13 January 1895 of Lord Leconfield's son, George, from typhoid.[161]

The 2nd Lord Leconfield inherited his family's love of field sports – a letter from Scotland to his wife at Petworth read: 'I have killed only 8 fish & lost 12 that were at the point of death. Thine, Henry. PS I enclose a fish'. He was also interested in the arts, not only as a

[below]
***The North Gallery*, by Hon. Mrs Percy (Madeline) Wyndham, *c.*1865.**
Gouache and watercolour on paper, 33.5 x 42.2 cm (no.706; North Gallery; Lord Egremont Collection)

builder, for he added highly important French furniture sold at the Hamilton Palace sale in 1882, most notably a Boulle commode (Red Room), an almost contemporary version of the pair designed and made by the royal *ébéniste,* André-Charles Boulle, for Louis XIV in 1708, and which is described in detail on page 139. According to his grandson, he was:

Handsome and grand
And idolised land.[162]

The 4th Lord Ribblesdale summarised his character:

He hardly ever spoke in the House, but his idol was Land in all its complexions and aspects. Cool, critical and shrewd, looking on the personal administration of great estates in Ireland and England as a profession, I can understand his being an awkward customer for a permanent official or a Minister. ... On Land he spoke from practical contact and knowledge, with authority.[163]

According to *The Complete Peerage,* he owned '66,000 acres in England and about 44,000 in Ireland – *viz.*, 30,221 acres in Sussex, 24,733 in Yorkshire, and 11,147 in Cumberland, besides 37,292 in Co. Clare, 6,269 in Co. Limerick, and 273 in Co. Tipperary. Total 109,935 acres, worth £88,112 a year... Lord Leconfield was one of the 28 noblemen, who in 1883 possessed above 100,000 acres in the United Kingdom and ranked 24th in order of acreage, though 10th in order of income'. He resented the fact that his father's bastardy had prevented him being an earl, but when an earldom was offered by Queen Victoria in 1886, he refused it, and afterwards 'was never quite the same'.[164]

He died, after a long illness, in London in 1901 (his widow, Constance, lived on until 1939) and was succeeded by his second son, Charles, whose long life connects the reign of Queen Victoria with the gift of Petworth to the National Trust in 1947. As a lieutenant in the 1st Life Guards, Charles was wounded in the South African War (1899–1902) and served in the First World War (as did his four younger brothers, one of whom was killed in action in 1914). In 1913, two years after their marriage, he and his wife Violet were painted by de Laszlo. Lord Leconfield's fashionable and punctilious dress in the portrait reveals the formal side of his character. His nephew and heir, John Wyndham, remembered that in the later 1930s:

Charles, 3rd Lord Leconfield and his wife Violet, Lady Leconfield, during a presentation at a hunt meet at Petworth in November 1936, on the occasion of their Silver Wedding

We had to dine in white tie and tails. When a gentleman came to stay with only a dinner jacket, and apologised for not having brought his tail-coat, Uncle Charles would offer what he thought the sage advice: 'You should sack your man'. It never entered his head that some of his guests might not have valets.[165]

His nephew thought him 'the kindest of men', but 'taciturn and gruff'. He was 'a great though morose trencherman', and 'ate so much that, after consultation with his physicians, he decided to restrict himself to huge breakfasts and huge dinners.... A baked egg and a glass of Madeira became his rule at luncheon. By the evening, quite ravenous, he would wander about the great house from room to room, staring out of rather bulbous eyes at his guests (if any), but saying nothing'. He was 'a unique character and a law unto himself', whose regime remained sybaritic during the Second World War:

In the winter of 1940, at the worst part of the war [wrote his nephew] I went down to Petworth to stay with Uncle Charles. The dinner was, of course, more austere than usual. Uncle Charles nevertheless drank a bottle of champagne himself and pressed me to do likewise. We then had some port, after which we had some brandy. Uncle Charles lit a cigar and his moroseness temporarily evaporated, as it always did after dinner. He suggested that we might go hunting next day, and I readily agreed. So out hunting we went: Uncle Charles, his huntsman, his whipper-in and me.... We found a fox and lost it, and while Uncle Charles's huntsman was casting for it we heard a tremendous hullabaloo about two miles away. Uncle Charles abused the huntsman and shouted at him: 'Can't you hear a holler?' and bade him, 'Get going thither.' So we galloped in the direction of the noise, only to find that it had nothing to do with fox-hunting: it was a village football match. The hounds, the huntsman, the whipper-in, Uncle Charles and I all slithered to a stop. The footballers and the bystanders who had been making the noise all stopped too. There was silence, then Uncle Charles, who had turned red in the face, stood up in his stirrups and shouted: 'Haven't you people got anything better to do in wartime than play *football*?'
We then went on hunting.[166]

The most unfortunate incidents during his reign of over 50 years were the sale (which he later regretted) of 13 important pictures in 1927, and the 'restoration' of several others in 1931 (thereafter he never allowed any of the pictures to be touched). The sale was engineered by a dealer masquerading as a hunting colonel, who profited from the huge demand for Old Masters (especially those with distinguished provenances) in America. The pictures included two Rembrandts, a Frans Hals, Holbein's portrait of Derich Berck, a Watteau and a Bronzino portrait (subsequently retrieved for Petworth by Lord Egremont). Lord Leconfield was persuaded that Kennedy North, a fashionable picture restorer who thought that impregnation with liquid wax was a panacea, should be entrusted with three Turners and the Le Nains' *Peasant Family* (no.48; Red Room). The results were disastrous, although there was some mitigation thanks to John Brealey, the conservator who was working for the Trust at Petworth in the early 1950s (he also rescued

Mantegna's *Triumphs of Caesar* at Hampton Court from Kennedy North's treatment). Although Brealey 'could not undo the damage, he was able to bring back much of the lost harmony'. The future of Petworth and its collections greatly exercised the mind of Lord Leconfield's heir, his nephew John Wyndham, whose elder brother, Henry, was killed at El Alamein in 1942. John Wyndham had spent the war as Harold Macmillan's right-hand man at the Ministry of Supply, the Colonial Office, in the Mediterranean and at the Air Ministry, and their connection was resumed in 1957, when Macmillan, by now Prime Minister, invited him to become his private secretary. John Wyndham's first-hand experience of Whitehall was to hold him in good stead during his frustrating negotiations with the Treasury over Petworth. Given the uncertain future for great houses, John Wyndham's first concern was to persuade Lord Leconfield of the advantages of the National Trust as Petworth's custodian:

> Before my uncle died [in 1952] I had pressed him to give Petworth and its park to the National Trust. I wanted to make sure that Petworth was preserved, and who could tell what the future might hold? I put this to Uncle Charles, and it was certainly one of the bravest things I've ever done. He could have struck me out of his will. Happily he didn't. But when he died I was faced with heavy death duties. Petworth House (and the park but not the estate) had already been given to the National Trust with the huge endowment sum of £300,000. It now occurred to me that some of the 700 pictures in the house might also be handed over in lieu of death duty, to remain on the walls where they belonged as the property of the nation.[167]

The house and the park were given to the Trust in 1947, when Lord Leconfield told James Lees-Milne, the Trust's Historic Buildings Secretary, that 'he was convinced he was wise in handing over to the National Trust'. Lees-Milne recorded a vignette of Petworth just emerging from its wartime chrysalis, occupied by the solitary Lord Leconfield and a skeleton staff:

> We lunched together (I not sent to the servants' hall). A large meal was left for us on hot stoves in the small dining-room. His kitchen is in the building over the way and his food has to pass underground. Promptly at 1.30 he summoned the nice old housekeeper and Moss, the house-carpenter, to take me round the house. All the pictures are now re-hung but the state-rooms are still under dust-sheets. Furniture in splendid condition, smelling of mansion polish and camphor. The housekeeper has

[left]
***A Peasant Family*, by Antoine, Louis and Mathieu Le Nain. The Le Nain brothers are best known for such unsentimental 'low-life' scenes. Painted in 1642, and inherited by the 3rd Earl from his uncle, the Earl of Thomond, in 1774.**
Oil on canvas, 76.5 x 88 cm. (no. 48; Red Room)

[below]
Osbert Lancaster's portrait of John Wyndham, 1st Lord Egremont, was used on the dust jacket of Wyndham's autobiography, *Wyndham and Children First,* 1968. The 1st Lord Egremont masterminded the complex negotiations that brought many of Petworth's contents to the National Trust, thus inaugurating the Acceptance in Lieu (of Tax) scheme that has since benefited numerous private owners and public institutions

one couple, the stableman and wife, who work in the house from 6.30 am to midday. Lord Leconfield joined us upstairs and waddled around. We made an odd little party. He is sweet with the servants, jokes with them in his funny, ponderous way. They however curiously subservient and rather sycophantic.[168]

John Wyndham's idea of offering pictures and other contents to the Treasury in lieu of the tax payable on the death of his uncle, Lord Leconfield, in 1953, is now an accepted procedure. But because this was the first time it had been mooted, the negotiations were tortuous and protracted. He began by writing a personal letter to the then Chancellor, R.A. Butler: 'There is no collection quite like it anywhere in the world today; and it oughtn't to be dispersed'. Butler applauded 'the imaginative offer', explained that an in lieu scheme was already under consideration, and John Wyndham went ahead:

Oh, what a mistake! I was the guinea-pig for the new plan. The plan was all right in principle: the Treasury would take over the stuff in lieu of death duties and arrange for the Trust to manage it. But the trouble and difficulty was in arriving at a fair price, for the Treasury had not been directly in the art market before.[169]

Another problem was that the government's expert advisers (the National Gallery for pictures) could not understand the Trust's desire to accept furnishing pictures of secondary importance but historical value. Nor did they always perceive the quality or importance of the paintings themselves. In the end, there was stalemate, and, as Lord Crawford, then Chairman of the Trust, complained to the permanent head of the Treasury: 'Owners won't face these obstacles and the years (three, I think in this case) of uncertainty and misery.... All I hope is that, if Petworth can be saved, a less disheartening procedure will be followed in future cases. Otherwise I am afraid that the idea of preserving country houses and their contents is dead.' The situation was only saved by John Wyndham's altruism in accepting the Treasury's net offer of £553,148: 'I have been hoping for a million pounds', he wrote, '...Whatever happens to me or my family, Petworth House, its contents and its park should be preserved for posterity. I am glad.'[170]

The Treasury's valuation was considered grossly unfair by Sir Anthony Blunt, Surveyor of the Queen's Pictures, who was involved in the negotiations on the Trust's behalf. As the Trust's Honorary Adviser on Paintings, he had already been responsible for a complete rearrangement of the pictures and had organised conservation work. Blunt's campaign began in 1952 after Lord Leconfield's death and before the house was opened to the public. Although the pictures 'had survived the rigours of Petworth remarkably well, especially considering that during the war the house was ... almost completely unheated', much essential conservation was required.[171] While this was in progress, Blunt embarked upon rehanging and rearranging pictures and sculpture

to a degree that he afterwards realised 'was in the end somewhat ruthless'. While eschewing 'a museum atmosphere', pictures were now arranged by subject – Van Dycks in the Square Dining Room, Turners in the 'Turner Room' (as the Red Room then became known) – and the 3rd Earl's miscellaneous arrangements ('a mixed bag', as Blunt put it), which had survived in several rooms, were unwittingly dismantled. To be fair to Blunt, he was unaware of the history of the collection's previous deployment; there had indeed been alterations since the 3rd Earl's death and his brief from the Trust was simply to 'see whether anything needed to be done about rehanging and cleaning'. In retrospect, he realised that he had broken with Petworth tradition 'to keep as far as possible the hanging arranged by the Third Earl'. But he did so with the blessing of the family, a fundamental principle of the Trust's management of its collections.

Following the 1947 gift of Petworth to the National Trust by the 3rd Lord Leconfield, the Wyndham family has continued the 800-year-old tradition of residence at Petworth. The south end of the house has always been the private apartment. The state rooms to the north have never been 'lived in', but were used both for grand entertainments and as an art gallery, which has been open to visitors since at least 1742. In 1963, after six years as Harold Macmillan's private secretary, John Wyndham was created 1st Lord Egremont, and in 1967 he succeeded his father as 6th Lord Leconfield.[172] His entertaining memoir of Petworth and of his own career, *Wyndham and Children First* (1968), records his years with Macmillan, whose 'Motto for Private Office and Cabinet' was 'Quiet, calm deliberation disentangles every knot'. In 1972 his elder son, Max, a biographer and novelist, succeeded him as 2nd Lord Egremont and 7th Lord Leconfield.

Since 1987 Lord and Lady Egremont have made generous loans of pictures to the Trust, enabling the spirit of the 3rd Earl's crowded picture hangs to be re-created. Once again, as in the Square Dining Room, the visitor can appreciate Petworth's interiors as Turner painted them, and in the North Gallery

Turner's landscapes can be seen not only top-lit on a red ground as he intended, but in relation to paintings by his contemporaries. These improvements to the interior of the house could only begin after 20 years of roof repairs (grant-aided by English Heritage) and related building works which rectified the structural instability of the first floor where huge timbers had been virtually eaten away by boring insects.

In the 1950s John Fowler had redecorated most of the public rooms for the Trust without reference to their historic treatment. This approach has been reversed in order to restore the original 19th-century schemes. The public rooms had become rather bare and formal after the 1950s, and again with the family's help, additional contents have been brought in to increase both the sense of grandeur and of domesticity. Lord and Lady Egremont have lent superb silver for the Square Dining Room, as well as the huge copper *batterie de cuisine* for the historic kitchen in the Servants' Quarters, opened to the public in 1995. A set of bedrooms, furnished and used by the family, has been open on weekdays since 1987. The work of redecoration and re-arrangement was made possible by a particularly generous anonymous benefactor and by other donations to the Trust.

The restoration of the Carved Room (completed in 2002) marked a high point in a decade of work which has been undertaken by the National Trust in partnership with Lord and Lady Egremont, and their adviser Alec Cobbe, who had helped to re-hang the private rooms along similar lines. The catalogue of the *Turner at Petworth* exhibition (2002) charts the depiction of pictures, furniture and décor by Turner and his fellow artists during what has been called Petworth's 'golden age'.[173] The exhibition, in partnership with Tate Britain, which was seen by 115,000 visitors in three months, involved the loan from the Tate of Turner's beautiful gouache sketches of Petworth, which recorded the look of the rooms filled with tier upon tier of pictures. The exhibition was unusual in that the Petworth rooms became not only a space to show the Turners and other paintings and drawings but also an intrinsic part of the display. The arrangement of pictures and furniture depicted by Turner in the early 19th century was restored as closely as possible. Indeed, as a result, Petworth may still be seen 'through Turner's eyes'.

[above]
Part of the Petworth copper *batterie de cuisine* on the Benham & Co gas range (*c.*1900)

[left]
The Wyndham and Leconfield families at Petworth in the 1930s. The 3rd Lord Leconfield (who bequeathed the house to the National Trust in 1947) stands to the right, next to his seated mother, Lady Constance (*née* Primrose), widow of the 2nd Lord Leconfield. The Dowager Lady Leconfield died in 1939, and the photograph seems to have been taken shortly before

[left below]
Some of the indoor servants seated in front of the Domestic Block in the 1880s: the French chef in the middle row

7

Pictures and sculpture

***The Adoration of the Magi*, attributed to Hieronymus Bosch (*c*.1450–1516), *c*.1515 (?). A possibly autograph variant of the central panel of Bosch's *Epiphany* triptych (Prado, Madrid).** Oil on panel, 100 x 73 cm (no.63; Somerset Room)

The number of pictures at Petworth is exceptional, amounting to well over 600, making up the largest single collection in a National Trust house. Their ownership is split between the National Trust and Lord Egremont, who generously loans many of them for display in the public rooms. Petworth also contains the largest Grand Tour collection of antique statuary still in its original setting, as well as early 19th-century British sculpture commissioned by the foremost champion of British sculptors, the 3rd Earl of Egremont. The rich history of Petworth and its owners is indivisible from its art collections, as previous chapters have shown. The intention here is to say something more about the character and intrinsic interest of individual pictures, groups of pictures, picture frames and sculpture. Because of the extent and quality of the Petworth collection – in effect a world-class museum set in the Sussex countryside – the choice is limited to a few representative artefacts which suggest themes and links between different phases of the collection's development.[174] Inevitably, given that there are 23 paintings by or after Van Dyck and 20 by Turner, these two very different artists share pride of place.

The picture collection at Petworth – in terms of art collecting rather than amassing miscellaneous portraits – was inaugurated during the reign of Charles I, the first sophisticated period of British connoisseurship, by Van Dyck's enthusiastic patron, Algernon Percy, 10th Earl of Northumberland, who was also a collector of Titian and other Old Masters. The painting at Petworth which is most redolent of the mid-17th-century approach to the collecting and display of art is *The Brussels Picture Gallery of the Archduke Leopold Wilhelm* (no.76; Somerset Room) by David Teniers the Younger (1610–90), which was purchased by the 2nd Earl of Egremont in 1756 at Prestage's auction room in London for the then-considerable sum of £241 (the second most expensive painting he bought).[175] Signed and dated 1651, only two years after Charles I's execution, it depicts numerous Old Master paintings

***The Brussels Picture Gallery of the Archduke Leopold Wilhelm* by David Teniers the Younger (1610–90), 1651.** Oil on canvas, 127 x 163 cm (no.76; Somerset Room)

from the Venetian Della Nave and Priuli collections, which had originally been sent to England for acquisition by the English crown. By 1639, however, Charles I was strapped for cash, so the Della Nave/Priuli pictures passed to the Royalist collector, James, 3rd Marquess and 1st Duke of Hamilton, who followed the king to the block on 9 March 1649. The first batch of 400 pictures bought by Archduke Leopold Wilhelm (1614–61) from the Hamilton collection was sent to Brussels in April 1649. Many are shown within his Brussels palace in Teniers's quintessential view of a picture gallery. The archduke was an arch-collector, with the means to buy extensively from an England recovering from civil war and dominated by a Puritan Commonwealth keen to sell off the royal collection for ready money. Teniers visited England in 1651, presumably in connection with the sales of crown property, though the archduke acquired only four pictures from Charles I's collection.

Teniers, known throughout Europe for his finely painted scenes of peasant life which served as models for Brussels tapestries, was an accomplished and sophisticated artist who served Leopold Wilhelm as curator. In 1660 he published in Antwerp – at his own expense – the first fully illustrated catalogue of a picture collection, the *Theatrum Pictorium*. It is dedicated to Leopold Wilhelm and documents the Old Masters that he had helped the archduke to acquire.[176] By then, Leopold Wilhelm had returned to Vienna with his pictures and in 1661 bequeathed them to his brother, the Holy Roman Emperor Ferdinand

III, which explains why most of the paintings depicted by Teniers in the Petworth picture are now among the chief ornaments of the Kunsthistorisches Museum, Vienna. A notable exception is at the top right: Titian's *Diana and Actaeon*, today in the National Gallery, London. Teniers made numerous small copies of the pictures on copper for the book engravers to work from. He also portrayed the archduke among his pictures and sculpture in a series of view paintings: the Petworth example is both one of the earliest and one of the most comprehensive.

Leopold Wilhelm's picture gallery was in the Coudenberg Palace in Brussels (severely damaged by fire in 1731 and later demolished), which was his seat as Spanish Governor-General of the South Netherlands (1647–56). His voracious appetite for good paintings was widely known, and – as well as buying from war-torn England – he bought many from the collection of the 1st Duke of Buckingham, when the 2nd Duke made them available in Antwerp in 1650.[177] Teniers's portrayal of the collection's highlights in a single room, hung closely together mainly in matching giltwood 'livery' frames, was an idealised representation, though typical of the picture-hanging style in contemporary princely galleries. The view through the window in the Petworth picture depicts the formal walled gardens of the Coudenberg Palace, which are delineated in an engraving of 1659. An engraving in the *Theatrum Pictorium* shows the actual arrangement after the archduke's return to Vienna in 1656 – the pictures were again hung in tiers and punctuated by sculpture, but in corridors around a courtyard in the Viennese Stallburg.[178] The caption reveals that the archduke owned 1,300 paintings and 268 pieces of sculpture: astonishing statistics!

By deciding upon an ideal depiction of the archducal gallery in the Petworth and other view paintings, Teniers was not only drawing upon the Flemish taste for such 'gallery' pictures, but was also anticipating the approach of Johan Zoffany in the 18th century, who adopted the same principles in his ideal depiction of the Uffizi Tribuna admired by prominent English Grand Tourists, painted for Queen Charlotte, consort of George III (*c.*1772–8; Royal Collection).[179] Teniers's fictive gallery – doubtless containing elements of the actual space, such as the high windows, the porch, the crowded hang and the furniture – is made more immediate by the inclusion of several portraits. There are three conversations going on: this is a living depiction of a gallery enjoyed as a repository of significant and beautiful things.[180] Four *valets-de-chambre* wearing short gowns and swords – including (far left) the High Chamberlain, Count Johan Adolf zu Schwarzenberg and the dwarfish archducal chaplain and painter of still-lifes, J. Antoine van der Baren – cluster around a table covered in drawings. Teniers, as curator, holds Annibale Carracci's oblong *Lamentation* upright on a crimson velvet chair, while the archduke chats to his guest, Antonius Triest, Bishop of Ghent, a fellow collector and Teniers's patron, who may well have commissioned, or have been given, the Petworth picture.

Modern conservation concerns are evident: some of the pictures have curtains which could be drawn to protect them from light and dust, just as the pictures in the Green Closet at Ham House were protected by green silk sarsenet curtains in 1677–83.[181] Double doors within a free-standing entrance porch ensure reasonable temperature and relative humidity control; while the large windows would have had secure shutters that also served to regulate the direction and amount of light. In galleries of this kind, where the paintings were hung cheek by jowl as 'wallpaper', they sometimes had to be brought down for closer scrutiny, where they might be placed on or against chairs and easels, as in Teniers's view. The archduke, who closely resembled Charles I, in black Spanish court dress, wears a sword and a broad hat in accordance with Spanish court etiquette (Teniers and the other courtiers are respectfully uncovered) and points with his cane to a portrait by Catena.

The classical statuary depicted by Teniers is complemented by a Florentine *pietre dure* table top (*c*.1597) supported by a bronze group of *Ganymede as Cupbearer with the Eagle of Jupiter*, made in the imperial foundry in Prague (1603–4). It was commissioned by the Emperor Rudolph II from the Dutch sculptor, Adriaen de Vries (1556–1626), and inherited by Archduke Leopold Wilhelm.[182] The complete table had arrived in Brussels by 1651, the date of Teniers's gallery picture, and – with Jupiter's eagle clearly also alluding to the armorial double-headed eagle of the Holy Roman Empire – was undeniably a symbol of notable artistic patronage within the Habsburg archduke's imperial family, as well as being a classic case of furniture as sculpture, entirely appropriate for a gallery. It is shown by Teniers in other depictions of Leopold Wilhelm's gallery, but has mysteriously disappeared without trace.[183]

Ganymede and the Eagle is a subject represented in the Petworth North Gallery by a classical statue (no.1; 2nd century AD) restored, as an engraving proves, for the 2nd Earl of Egremont by the famous 18th-century Roman restorer Bartolomeo Cavaceppi. The statue still retains Cavaceppi's toning designed to hide the restorations he had made to the fragmentary and dirty original. The survival of the toning, including etching with hydrochloric acid, is exceptional, allowing a fuller appreciation of the restorer's subtle intentions.[184]

The overall impression of the archducal gallery is of an overcrowded, but none the less impressive *mise-en-scène*, in which the juxtaposition of pictures, sculpture and drawings conveys strong messages, both about the character of the collection and about the determined acquisitiveness of its patron, who owned no fewer than 517 High Renaissance Italian pictures. These were the 'French Impressionists' of that era, but unlike some rich collectors today, there was no doubt about the archduke's good taste (or indeed about his impeccable credentials). Teniers's sophisticated conversation piece celebrates the archduke's love of High Renaissance art and his pleasure in collecting. This must have been why it appealed to the 2nd Earl of Egremont, who shared the archduke's Italian tastes in pictures and sculpture, and who arranged Egremont House in impeccable style as a showcase for his numerous Old Masters.[185]

We know from various accounts that the 2nd and 3rd Earls of Egremont also delighted in showing off their collections. The former at Egremont House, which was designed for grand entertainment, and the latter at Petworth, in his own idiosyncratic and diffident manner. Many conversations between the 3rd Earl's artistic friends took place among the pictures and sculpture, just as Teniers depicts the archducal collection as a living entity. Some of Turner's sketch views show both painters and visitors. The 3rd Earl was very keen for artists to record his arrangements, especially in the 1820s, when Turner was most active there, and in 1835 Henry Wyndham Phillips (son of Thomas Phillips, the painter) recorded the layout of the North Gallery sculpture and listed the pictures. There are also diagrammatic records of the picture hangs throughout the house (*c.*1840–3), as well as an anonymous printed picture catalogue (by A.E. Knox, 1856).[186] The Petworth pictures were hung thickly and randomly in symmetrical tiers, and artists were allowed to take paintings down in order to study or copy them, or even to hang them in their bedrooms.

The North Gallery, where Teniers's *Brussels Picture Gallery of the Archduke Leopold Wilhelm* was hanging in 1835, was filled – if not quite so tightly as the archducal gallery –with a mélange of Old Masters and contemporary pictures as well as both antique and modern sculpture. Indeed, the 3rd Earl of Egremont was portrayed posthumously at whole length 'as when about sixty years old' by his own equivalent to Teniers as 'in-house' painter, Thomas Phillips (1770–1845), the author of numerous portraits at Petworth. Egremont is represented seated on a sofa in the North Gallery with the colossal *Venus, Vulcan and Cupid* (1827/8–31) by his 'in-house' sculptor, John Edward Carew, and Flaxman's *St Michael overcoming Satan* (1819–26) prominent in the background, exactly as they are today following the restoration and rearrangement of the North Gallery in 1992–3. Hanging in the Square Bay, built by the 3rd Earl as a suitable receptacle for Flaxman's masterpiece, Phillips depicts paintings commissioned from his and Egremont's mutual friends, including Hilton, Leslie and Turner. As in Teniers's painting, which shows a small equestrian bronze of the archduke on the table, Lord Egremont rests his hand on a carpet-covered table supporting a silver gilt racing cup by Rebecca Emes, won in 1825 at Goodwood by Cricketer, the horse commemorated by the

[left]
The North or Square Bay of the North Gallery, built to display Flaxman's *St Michael overcoming Satan* (completed 1826), which is surrounded by statues by John Edward Carew

[left below]
***St Michael overcoming Satan* by John Flaxman (1755–1826), 1819–26.** Marble, 344 cm high (no.97; North Gallery)

[right]
The 'Leconfield Aphrodite', attributed to Praxiteles (*c*.400-*c*.330 BC), *c*.330 BC. Parian marble, 64 cm high (no.73; Red Room)

bronze statuette. The spine of the folio propped against the sofa reveals a love of Italian art – tellingly, the earl's favourite painters were Raphael and Hogarth – while at his feet lies one of his beloved spaniels, just as the archduke is depicted with two of his brown and white dogs.

Like the 3rd Earl's father, the 2nd Earl of Egremont, the archduke was an avid collector of antique sculpture, which takes second place in Teniers's depiction of his gallery. The great masterpiece of antique and modern sculpture at Petworth, the so-called 'Leconfield Aphrodite', is a signal rarity. Its head, which originally belonged to a full-length statue, is comparable in style to the *Aphrodite of Knidos* and the *Venus de' Medici*, Its attribution to Praxiteles, the most famous of all Greek sculptors, or to his school at the very least, has stood the test of time. Furtwängler wrote in 1888: 'I was absolutely enraptured by its beauty ... this is a real original by one of the first fourth-century [BC] artists ... of the period of Praxiteles.' Sculpture of this early date was imitated widely in the Roman world, but there is something in the dreaminess of the eyes, the treatment of the hair and the ineffable beauty of the 'Leconfield Aphrodite' that leads one to conclude that it is indeed 'from Praxiteles's school if not his hand'.[187]

The purchase of Teniers's painting in 1756 by the 2nd Earl of Egremont, and its display first among the pictures in Egremont House, and then with the multitudinous pictures and sculpture in the North Gallery at Petworth by his son, the 3rd Earl, emphasise that the Percy /Seymour/Wyndham family 'gallery' – meaning the collection as a whole – may be firmly placed in the great tradition of European collecting. The high status of the Petworth 'gallery' in terms of High Renaissance art would have been more evident before the split of the Petworth inheritance in 1750 on the death of the 7th Duke of Somerset, and before the departure from Petworth of Titian's *The Vendramin Family*, the jewel of the 10th Earl of Northumberland's collection, and the dispersal of 13 important Old Masters, including a Holbein and two Rembrandts, in 1927. Even so, Petworth still houses two paintings originally attributed to Titian (one fully autograph), the eight little Elsheimers, and two Andrea del Sartos from the 10th Earl's collection. Teniers's immortal image of the archduke among his paintings and sculpture (sadly, a type of picture that was a rarity at the time and indeed subsequently) may well have inspired the 2nd Earl of Egremont to increase his purchases of Old Masters (he bought some 200), just as it may have encouraged his son, the 3rd Earl, to give Turner the opportunity to paint the house, its park and – in his sketches – the diurnal life of the Petworth 'gallery'.

Petworth is home to 23 Van Dycks – all bar two acquired by the 10th Earl of Northumberland mainly from the artist – which were a considerable inspiration to Turner and his contemporaries in the 1820s, nearly 200 years after Van Dyck's death. They appear in many of Turner's gouaches-cum-watercolours of the state rooms, notably his view of the White and Gold Room, which was hung – as it still is today – with four of Van Dyck's female portraits.[188] These are truly ravishing pictures. The palm is generally given to *Lady Anne Carr, Countess of Bedford* (*c.*1638; Lord Egremont Collection), which the mercurial Benjamin Robert Haydon described in 1826 'as the finest Vandyke in the world', and of which Turner made a free copy. The late Sir Oliver Millar thought the *Anne Carr* was 'one of Van Dyck's most magical portraits', praising the 'momentary frozen movement in the hands' as she puts off a leather glove and 'imperceptibly moves forward'.[189] Lady Anne is dressed in the height of fashion, wearing the large pearls that were then *de rigueur*, while her slight double chin and plumpness was considered the acme of female beauty, as can be seen in Van Dyck's

***Lady Anne Carr, Countess of Bedford*, by Sir Anthony Van Dyck (1599–1641), *c.*1638.** Oil on canvas, 136.2 x 109.9 cm (no.220; White and Gold Room; Lord Egremont Collection)

***Mountjoy Blount, 1st Earl of Newport, Lord George Goring and a Page,* by Sir Anthony Van Dyck (1599–1641).** Oil on canvas, 135 x 180 cm (no.289; Square Dining Room)

other portraits of beautiful women at Petworth.[190] Above all, the painting is in superb condition, and all four Van Dyck countesses in the White and Gold Room probably retain the matching carved giltwood frames that the 10th Earl of Northumberland, who had a *penchant* for Van Dyck's female portraits, applied in the 1660s to 11 of his Van Dycks.[191] Turner sketched a copy of another of the Van Dyck portraits (of the 10th Earl's sister, *Lady Lucy Percy, Countess of Carlisle,* dipping her right hand into a fountain; now in the Little Dining Room)[192] and was also clearly fascinated not only by the quality of Petworth's ancestral collection but also by the sheer number of pictures and the beauty of their multi-tiered symmetrical arrangement, as is evident most particularly in his view of the Square Dining Room.

As Turner shows, the Square Dining Room is another famous repository of Van Dyck portraits, and the hang depicted in his sketch view has been recreated in its essentials.[193] Here, on the west wall, hang the two double portraits of *Algernon Percy, 10th Earl of Northumberland* and his family and of *Mountjoy Blount, 1st Earl of Newport, Lord George Goring and a Page,* flanking the door into the Marble Hall. Turner only depicts the former, which is a touching representation of Van Dyck's patron, his wife and daughter, painted *c.*1634. Either side of the Square Dining Room chimneypiece are two more Van Dycks: *Henry, Baron Percy of Alnwick,* and the posthumous portrait of *Henry Percy, 9th Earl of Northumberland,* painted for his son, the 10th Earl.

Thomas Wentworth, 1st Earl of Strafford **by Sir Anthony Van Dyck (1599–1641), 1636.**
Oil on canvas, 134 x 109 cm (no.311; Little Dining Room)

In the Little Dining Room, traditionally called 'The Vandyke Room', is another cluster of Van Dyck's masterpieces, including the paramount version of his portrait of the ill-fated *Earl of Strafford*, Charles I's distinguished minister and Van Dyck's patron, betrayed and beheaded in 1641, and the portrait of *Catherine Bruce, Mrs William Murray* (no.295), who was the chatelaine of Ham House (NT). Over the chimneypiece is *St Sebastian* by Gerard Seghers (1591–1651), an Antwerp artist influenced by Van Dyck, who also acted as a picture agent for Archduke Leopold Wilhelm. The frame is a rare survival from the 1660s, retaining its original ebonised and silvered decoration, and of added interest as probably the choice of the 10th Earl, who certainly acquired Seghers's recently restored painting.

The significance of 'Lord Egremont's gallery' was recognised by collectors, pundits and by one of the greatest of contemporary painters, John Constable, who described Petworth as 'that house of art', declaring that its surrounding landscape was of even greater inspiration to him than either the famous 'Petworth Claude' or Ruisdael's *Waterfall* (no.48*; Somerset Room). Most of Turner's late 1820s views of the rooms were painted for his own amusement – and doubtless for the pleasure of his host, the 3rd Earl, and of his fellow-guests – concurrently with the earl's imaginative commission to paint the four magnificent landscapes,

St Sebastian **by Gerard Seghers (1591–1651).**
Oil on canvas, 216 x 142 cm (no.601; Little Dining Room; Lord Egremont Collection)

executed *con amore* in Turner's private Petworth studio, which were returned in 2002 to their original setting in the panelling of Grinling Gibbons's Carved Room, thus recreating an arrangement partly devised by Turner himself.

Turner and his friends revelled in the historic collection, which – together with the sheer beauty of the place – inspired some of Turner's greatest landscapes. The Proud Duke's 'Petworth Claude', *Landscape with Jacob and Laban and his Daughters* (*c*.1654; no.329; Somerset Room) was virtually copied by Turner in his *Apullia in Search of Appullus – Vide Ovid* (1814; Tate Britain), just as Turner's *The Fall of an Avalanche in the Grisons* (1810; Tate) was inspired by de Loutherbourg's *Storm and Avalanche, near the Scheideck* (no.362) at Petworth. However, it was Turner's reaction to the park, the wider landscape (recorded like the house in his numerous sketches) and the Petworth way of life which inspired two of his supreme landscapes, painted for the Carved Room and probably completed in 1830.[194] Still in good condition and very freely painted, in Gibbons-style frames carved by Jonathan Ritson, they were fixed, with two other landscapes, into the panelling at a comparatively low level – idiosyncratically and eccentrically beneath full-length dynastic portraits and Gibbons's masterly carvings – so that guests at Egremont's festive board could sit comfortably and look from the pictures to 'Capability' Brown's 1760s landscape through the high windows. Sadly, most of us cannot enjoy great art from such a position of comfort, but Egremont's motley collection of guests was able to do so, and this must have been one of the reasons for the commission. Such care was taken over the final effect that Turner not only referred to pencil and watercolour sketches but also painted trial versions in oil (Tate), which were fixed into the panelling to allow the earl to comment and the artist to refine.[195]

***Storm and Avalanche near the Scheideck*, by Philip James de Loutherbourg (1740–1812).** Oil on canvas, 107 x 157.5 cm (no.362; Red Room)

Turner will almost certainly have finished off the final versions *in situ* as he famously was wont to do on Varnishing Days, immediately before the opening of the Royal Academy's exhibitions.[196]

Two of the four Carved Room landscapes depict Petworth park from the house: the first with a broader perspective incorporating a cricket match, the second from closer to the lake. In the former picture, the sun is setting over the lake in fiery tones, while the dying light catches the iridescence of the water, the whites of the cricketers, the sleek coats of the deer and the antlers of the stags. In the second painting, the landscape dissolves as the sun is about to dip below the trees on the far ridge towards Tillington and is reflected like a Naples yellow ball in the rippling water, with its white swans, black moorhens and drinking deer. These two paintings constitute Turner's most poetic tribute to the Petworth he loved and to the lake on which he passed many a happy hour, observing the fleeting changes of the light and the weather, while fishing for large pike, sometimes with his friend, Sir Francis Chantrey.

The American-born Charles Robert Leslie (1794–1859) was another artist who became a close friend of the 3rd Earl and who also painted the interior of the house, as well as – like Turner – including reminiscences of it in his history pictures taken from literary subjects. Indeed, Leslie was successful in rising to Egremont's challenge to paint 'history' pictures in the European grand tradition. Leslie's fellows – including Chantrey, one of the foremost sculptors of the day – usually proved unable to release themselves from the tyranny of portraiture or failed in their attempts to achieve the grand manner: sometimes failing spectacularly, as in Haydon's *Alexander taming Bucephalus* (no.660; North Gallery; Lord Egremont Collection). Leslie's scenes taken from literature and history, and painted with a refined beauty of execution in the manner of the Dutch 17th-century *fijnschilders* [fine painters], provide unexpected revelations, given that this style of painting is still unappreciated. Leslie himself, famous in his own day, is generally forgotten, but deserves a revival of interest and scholarly attention. Two of his best pictures now hang in the North Gallery: *Sancho and the Duchess* (1824), which Creevey thought was 'the cleverest and prettiest thing I ever saw',[197] and its later companion, painted as a pendant, *Gulliver Presented to the Queen of Brobdignag* (1835). The first is taken from Cervantes's *Don Quixote* (1605 and 1615), the latter from Swift's *Gulliver's Travels* (1727). Other similar paintings are *Catherine and Petruchio* (no.134; Lord Egremont Collection), and *Charles II and Lady Margaret Bellenden* and *Lucy Percy, Countess of Carlisle, bringing the Pardon to her Father* (nos.221, 224; Lord Egremont Collection), which were hung by the 3rd Earl below the Van Dyck 'countesses' in the White and Gold Room, as depicted in Turner's watercolour view.[198] Leslie's small oil of the Carved Room (*c.*1828; Tate) is one of the most beautiful evocations of a room at Petworth.[199] It was adapted many years later for *The Heiress* (exh. RA, 1845, no.131; Leger Galleries, London, 1968, no.29). Leslie also painted watercolour views of Petworth interiors.[200] His published memoir is a useful source for artistic life at Petworth and contains valuable examples of the 3rd Earl's behaviour as a patron.[201]

The Lake in Petworth Park or _The Lake, Petworth: Sunset, a Stag drinking_ by J.M.W. Turner (1775–1851), _c._1829. Oil on canvas, 63.5 x 132 cm (no.142; Carved Room). (Tate)

One of Turner's watercolours-cum-gouaches depicts the Red Room, named after the colour of its walls, in which pride of place is once again given – since the 2002 recreation of Turner's view by redecoration and rehanging – to Van Dyck's full-length portraits of *Sir Robert Shirley* and *Lady Shirley* (nos.96–7). Painted in 1622, both were first listed at Petworth in 1764, which suggests that they were probably acquired by the 2nd Earl of Egremont.[202] The other Van Dycks at Petworth were painted in his English period (1632–42), but although this exceptional pair of portraits is of an Englishman and his wife, they are completely atypical, standing almost alone in his *oeuvre*, and most akin to his master Rubens's flamboyant portraits of the Genoese aristocracy. Even the painstaking German connoisseur, Gustav Waagen, doubted them in 1854 on the basis that they were 'too feeble in drawing and too heavy in colour for Vandyck'.[203] On the contrary, the exotic Persian clothing and

***The Red Room*, by J.M.W. Turner (1775–1851), *c*.1827.** Gouache, 14 x 19 cm. (Tate)

Sir Robert Shirley (1581–1628) **by Sir Anthony Van Dyck (1599–1641), painted in Rome in 1622. Shirley was the ambassador to Pope Gregory XV of Shah Abbas II 'the Great' of Persia.** Oil on canvas, 214 x 129 cm (no.96; Red Room)

Teresia, Lady Shirley **by Sir Anthony Van Dyck (1599–1641), 1622.** Oil on canvas, 214 x 129 cm (no.97; Red Room)

accoutrements, together with the beauty of Lady Shirley, inspired Van Dyck to virtuoso performances. Van Dyck met the Shirleys in Rome, during Sir Robert's brief ambassadorship as envoy of Shah Abbas II 'the Great' of Persia to Pope Gregory XV (22 July–29 August 1622). He made three drawings of the couple in his *Italian Sketchbook*, noting on the drawing of Lady Shirley that she had the *habito et maniera di Persia* ['the clothes and manner of Persia'].[204]

Sir Robert was one of the most cosmopolitan Englishmen of his day. From Whiston in Sussex, where their father built a large house with his nefarious profits as Treasurer at War in the Low Countries, he and his elder brother, Sir Anthony Shirley (as British envoy), travelled to Persia in 1598. By 1607 Robert had married Teresia Khan, a noble Circassian Christian. The Shirleys travelled together on his Persian embassy to Europe, seeking trade agreements and anti-Turkish support. He received titles and presents, was knighted at the imperial court of Rudolf II in Prague, and also visited Poland, Florence, the Vatican and Madrid, arriving in London in 1611 to a warm welcome from James I. Here, Teresia bore a son, Henry, whose godfather was no less than Henry, Prince of Wales. The Shirleys then returned to Persia, re-appearing in Madrid (1617–22). It was on a brief stop in Rome in 1622 *en route* to England again that he and his wife were painted by Van Dyck. Shirley is portrayed standing, as Persian Ambassador, with his

***Rider and Herdsmen in an Imaginary Landscape with a Ruined Castle and Distant Town* by Aelbert Cuyp (1620–91), *c.*1650–9.** Oil on canvas, 104.7 x 176 cm (no.114; Beauty Room)

turban held in place by a jewelled *aigrette*, bearing a bow and quiver of arrows presumably as a symbol of status (European courtiers then wore swords). His cloth-of-gold cloak is heavily embroidered in Persian style. Lady Shirley is seated *à la persane* as an exotic denizen of a fabulous country that was then almost unknown to Europeans. She sits on a Persian carpet, resting on cushions, with an ebony gilt-mounted Italian dressing glass face-up on a blue-and-gold, damask-covered low table. Her elegant be-ringed hands in her lap, she faces the spectator with a quizzical and amused look enhanced by the sinuous line of her eyebrows and by her sparkling eyes, which seem to reveal both intelligence and curiosity. Her hair is swept back, falling to the sides in ringlets, and is anchored, together with her overarching veil, by a black feathered *aigrette*. She wears a pearl necklace and a stomacher of jewels hanging from a gold chain. Shirley died in Persia in 1628, and Lady Shirley returned to Rome, where she died 40 years later in a convent.

The frames of the Shirley Van Dycks were made by Samuel Norman (active 1746–67), the 2nd Earl of Egremont's major contractor for the furnishing and decoration of Egremont House and one of the most expensive cabinetmakers in London. Among his other documented frames at Petworth are Kneller's full-length *Queen Anne* (no.208; Beauty Room), supplied in 1763 for £23 2s,[205] and Sébastien Bourdon's *The Selling of Joseph* (no.18; Red Room), probably the 'very neat Picture frame to match an old one, with Sweep Corners & middles' for which Norman was paid four guineas in 1762.[206] Norman's frames were inspired by French frames, just as his flamboyant seat furniture was in French style.

A particularly magnificent Parisian frame, acquired with the picture by the 2nd Earl, is that of the *Landscape with Troglodyte Goatherds* (*c.*1610–

15; no.83; Somerset Room) by the Antwerp painter, Paul Bril (1554–1626). The frame was presumably made in 1730 when the picture was acquired by Jacques-François-Léonor de Goyan-Matignon, duc de Valentinois (1689–1751). In a developed post-Régence style, it is notable for the crispness of the carving, and the preservation of much of its original burnished and matt gilding. The presence of carved centres as well as corner shells adds to its grandeur, as does the precise cutting of acanthus, vegetal and geometric decoration, which is distinguished by fluid and sinuous movement. This is the sort of frame that inspired Samuel Norman's French-style work, as can also be seen around another purchase of the 2nd Earl, Snyders's large *Concert of Birds* (no.161; Oak Hall). The set of little Elsheimers was also reframed in more delicate Rococo style by Joseph Duffour, a Frenchman based in

***Landscape with Troglodyte Goatherds*, by Paul Bril (1554–1626), *c.*1610–15.** Oil on canvas, 112 x 142 cm; in a carved and gilded frame, Paris, *c.*1730 (no.83; Somerset Room)

London, for the 2nd Earl in 1752. The attractive frames were appropriate for their transfer to Lady Egremont's dressing room at Egremont House.

Bril's landscape was bought by the 2nd Earl in 1754 on the London market. Its style represents the artist's transitional period in Rome, when he was increasingly influenced by Annibale Carracci's naturalistic landscape painting, and when he was painting on canvas on a much larger scale than his previous cabinet pictures on copper. Adam Elsheimer's slightly earlier jewel-like depictions of saints in lush landscape backgrounds, *Saints and Prophets from the Old and New Testaments* (*c.*1605; nos.272–9; Somerset Room), also make interesting comparisons with Claude's large *Landscape* hanging nearby. Like the Bril, they

***The Capitol with Santa Maria d'Aracoeli, Rome,* by Bernardo Bellotto (*c.*1721–80).** Oil on canvas, 86.4 x 148.6 cm (no.667; Somerset Room)

represent earlier evocations of the Italian *campagna* and its limpid light, which Claude – with his matchless poetry – elevated to the status of great art. The Italian landscape and Claude's interpretation of it were also to influence a subsequent generation of Dutch and Flemish painters, such as Aelbert Cuyp (1620–91) whose *Rider and Herdsman in an Imaginary Landscape with a Ruined Castle and Distant Town* (*c.*1655; no.114; Beauty Room) is bathed in golden Italian light. Dutch landscape is also represented in the Somerset Room by both native and Germanic scenes in the tranquil *Landscape with a Coppice* (no.15) by Meindert Hobbema and a vigorous example of a *Waterfall* by Jacob Ruisdael (no.48*). *The Capitol, Rome* (*c.*1742; no.667; Somerset Room) by Bernardo Bellotto (*c.*1721–80) is a rarity in a British collection, where the landscapes of his uncle, Canaletto, are widespread. This is probably the 'View in Rome' by 'Canaletti', inherited in 1774 by the 3rd Earl from his uncle, the Earl of Thomond. It shows the Campidoglio, designed by Michelangelo around the ancient bronze equestrian statue of Marcus Aurelius.

The Petworth collection contains a group of Early Netherlandish pictures, including two fragments attributed to Rogier van der Weyden (mainly Little Dining Room), which are rare in British country house collections. The star piece is *The Adoration of the Magi* (*c.*1515 (?); no.63; Somerset Room) attributed to Hieronymus Bosch (*c.*1450–1516). It is a possibly autograph variant of the central panel of Bosch's triptych of the *Epiphany* (Prado, Madrid), painted for the cathedral of s'-Hertogenbosch and acquired in 1574 by Philip II of Spain.

This *tour d'horizon* of Petworth's paintings ends with a final homage to the 3rd Earl's patronage. After his death in 1837, collecting at Petworth did not come to a halt, but what is still felt to have been the 'golden age' of the house drew to a close. The subsequent late Victorian alterations to the fabric of the rooms (notably the partial dismantling of the Carved Room) and the 1950s thinning of the crowded hangs of pictures were reversed in 1992–2002, so that Petworth can once again be seen through the eyes of the 3rd Earl and his friends. The North Gallery, which he extended in the late 1820s, was restored in 1992–3, so that the pictures could be appreciated in natural toplighting (the skylights were rebuilt to the original specifications, with electric blinds to control and direct the light). Here hangs, in the centre of the west wall on a red ground as in Turner's own gallery, his 'Egremont Seapiece': *Ships Bearing up for Anchorage* (no.33). The numerous preliminary studies for this early masterpiece indicate Turner's search for perfection in the depiction of 'ships sailing, coming up into the wind, shortening sail and dropping anchor'. Arguably the greatest of the many Turners at Petworth, being able to see it close up and in natural light is a revelation, especially as Turner can be seen in the North Gallery in relation to his other landscapes and those of his contemporaries.

***Ships Bearing up for Anchorage (the 'Egremont Seapiece')*, by J.M.W. Turner (1775–1851), exhibited 1802.** Oil on canvas, 112 x 180.3 cm (no.33; North Gallery). (Tate)

The painting bears its original gallery frame, just as the North Gallery is distinctive for the numerous giltwood frames around the pictures commissioned by the 3rd Earl, some plain, some flamboyantly decorated both by carving in wood and composition. Further research will doubtless reveal much about the London picture framers of the day.

In the North Gallery's Central Corridor hangs a memorial to a great event at Petworth, recorded by Thomas Phillips (1770–1845) in his masterpiece: *The Allied Sovereigns at Petworth, 24 June 1814* (1817; no.268). The 3rd Earl welcomes a future king, an emperor, and another king: his friend the Prince Regent, Tsar Alexander I and King Friedrich Wilhelm III of Prussia. Both the Tsar and the Prussian king had been defeated by Napoleon (the latter ignominiously) and this gathering was a preliminary – as it turned out – to the Waterloo campaign, in which the 3rd Earl's second son, General Sir Henry Wyndham, distinguished himself, as he had done at Vittoria the previous year. The victories of Vittoria and Waterloo were later to be celebrated at Petworth in the paintings by George Jones (nos.198 and 200; Beauty Room) and in the earl's adaptation of the Beauty Room as a patriotic shrine.

In the plethora of portraits in Phillips's *Allied Sovereigns*, Petworth ascends the national stage, but it was not Egremont's preferred *modus vivendi*. He was at his happiest, as Creevey memorably described him in 1828, passing his life 'in eternal locomotion from one room to another without sitting for an instant', favouring 'a life of enjoyment to one of celebrity'. Creevey was amused by the evidence of Egremont's past *amours* in the portraits, but above all it was the magnitude of the collection and the scale of the rooms which enraptured him. Today, it is once again possible to enjoy this early 19th-century picture and sculpture paradise much as it was when Creevey recorded his first impressions in August 1828: 'the infinity of pictures [and] statues throughout made as agreeable an impression upon me as I ever witnessed'.[207]

***The Allied Sovereigns at Petworth, 24 June 1814* by Thomas Phillips (1770–1845), 1817.** Oil on canvas, 127 x 137.2 cm (no.268; North Gallery)

8

Furniture and woodwork

Sarcophagus-shaped commode (detail of Sphinx corner mount), by André-Charles Boulle (1642–1732) and workshop, *c.*1710 (Red Room)

Not surprisingly – given the exceptional grandeur and extent of its varied collections – Petworth contains highly important, well-documented and beautiful furniture, which has tended to take third place to the National Trust's finest single collections of paintings and sculpture. The earliest pieces of furniture in any National Trust house are three marble table legs, *c.*200 AD, converted in the 19th century into bow-fronted single-legged tables for the support of antique marble busts (North Gallery). These three *trapezephora* in the form of griffons (lions with goat's horns) with leonine feet were originally elements of antique Roman centre- or side-tables.[208] Like most of the other Petworth marbles, they were probably acquired in Italy *c.*1760–63 for the 2nd Earl of Egremont.

In the medieval Chapel stands one of the earliest indigenous brass lecterns in a British country house. It was bought for £3 2s 6d on 7 April 1582 by the 8th Earl of Northumberland[209] and seems rather earlier in style. A similar, larger eagle lectern, also with three feet in the form of crouching lions, is in the Chapel at Eton College (completed 1482) and is thought to be part of its original furnishings.

In the North Gallery is the terrestrial globe, London, 1592, by Emery Molyneux (d.1598–9), which is the earliest surviving English globe, unvarnished to this day and still supported by its original turned and painted wooden stand.[210] It is said to have been given to the 9th Earl of Northumberland by Sir Walter Ralegh, when they were both imprisoned in the Tower. It was certainly kept in the Tower, but Northumberland may have acquired the globe earlier around the date of its publication in 1592. The *Tractatus de Globis et eorum Usu* (1594; dedicated to Ralegh), a guide to the use of the Molyneux globes, was written by Robert Hues, who was later in Northumberland's service. Given that Northumberland was described in 1635 as 'the favourer of all good learning, and Maecenas of learned men',[211] he may have provided financial backing to Molyneux's development of the globes.

Terrestrial globe, 1592, by Emery Molyneux (d.1598–9). Wood, brass, and engraved and painted paper applied to plaster, weighted with sand. Globe 80 cm in diameter. (North Gallery)

Eagle lectern, Flemish or English, *c*.1480 (?), bought in 1582 by the 8th Earl of Northumberland. Brass, 165 cm high. (Chapel)

Molyneux was at the cutting edge of geography at the time: his globe was based upon voyages of discovery with Francis Drake. The navigations of Drake, Cavendish and Frobisher are traced on the globe, which is elaborately decorated with cartouches, fanciful sea-monsters and other marine fantasies by the Fleming, Jodocus Hondius (1563–1611), who subsequently pirated his engravings for Molyneux in the production of identical globes under his own name in Holland. The Petworth globe is dedicated to Queen Elizabeth I, who described Molyneux's globe as the 'whole earth, a present for a Prince; but with the Spanish King's leave'. The memory of England's narrow escape from invasion in 1588 by the world superpower of the day was still clearly in her mind.

When the 9th Earl died in 1632, his Library at Petworth contained 'one large globe and two small ones'. The 'large globe' must be the one by Molyneux; the other two smaller ones must be the pair of library globes (1616–17), by Willem Jansz. Blaeu (*c*.1571–1638), sold in 1968 from Petworth.[212] They reveal that the 9th Earl continued to acquire the most up-to-date globes as geographical knowledge expanded.

In the centre of the Somerset Room stands a carved walnut centre-table, made in Florence, *c*.1580. The top has been replaced, and the polished walnut was presumably once partly gilded in typical Italian fashion. The end sections bear central cartouches carved with three Percy crescents, flanked by boldly carved volutes and by bare-breasted female caryatids, whose bodies meld into larger-scale paw feet. The 1632 inventory reveals that there were sets of tapestries, including those in the 9th Earl's bedroom, which were woven with 'halfe moones' (the Percy crescent device). The concept of the table is typically Mannerist Italian, of the mid-16th century, a style that was influenced by the engraved furniture designs (*c*.1560) of Northerners like Jacques I Androuet Du Cerceau. Indeed these caryatids are out of the same stable as the 'sea-dogs' (female sea-lions) of the famous 'sea-dog table', France, *c*.1580, at Hardwick (NT), which was also originally partly gilded. The Petworth table was probably commissioned by the 9th Earl, who was in Italy in the 1580s and who owned books by Du Cerceau and Vredeman de Vries.[213] A partly gilded Roman table with a *pietre dure* top (V & A, London) is supported by comparable caryatids blending into paw feet.[214] The Petworth table may well have been designed to support a similar top of *pietre dure*.

The two sets of nine *sgabelli* or backstools, North Italian, probably Tuscany, *c*.1600 (Grand Staircase), were probably intended for Northumberland House, the Percys' London palace. First listed at Petworth in 1680, in the 'Lobby', the backstools had moved to the Marble Hall in 1750, when they were described as 'eighteen carved and gilt wood [chairs] with halfe moons'.[215] They were then most likely

***Sgabelli* from a set of nine, North Italy, probably Tuscany, *c.*1600.** Walnut (originally partly gilded), ebonised before 1764

partly gilded, with much of the walnut unpainted. The 'halfe moons' refer to the Percy crescent, which is painted onto the backs of one set of nine; the backs of the other set being carved in the form of shells, with a grotesque head at the base instead of a cartouche for armorials. They were presumably partly ebonised before 1764, when 'Twelve Black & Gilt hall Chairs' were recorded in a vestibule adjoining the Marble Hall.

The two candidates for their commission or acquisition are the 9th and 10th Earls of Northumberland. The latter visited France, Holland and Italy (1619–24) and is known to have bought 'backstooles of the Italian fashion' in 1636. The Petworth *sgabelli* have been linked to the 10th Earl's 1636 purchase, and described as English in Italian style, like a set of six at Lacock Abbey (NT) and a pair of similar painted armchairs, of which one is in the V&A.[216] Both sets of Petworth *sgabelli* are in fact Italian. A pair of Italian *sgabelli* in the V&A carved with similar *putti* heads and feet are dated *c.*1580–1600, which suggests that the Petworth *sgabelli* actually may have been acquired by the 9th Earl before his return from the Continent in 1584.[217]

Much more furniture survives from the period 1692–1748, when Petworth was transformed into a Franco-Dutch palace by the 'Proud' 6th Duke of Somerset with the advice of William III's *ornemaniste* Daniel Marot. The panelling of the Marble Hall (the original state entrance in .the centre of the park front, largely completed in 1692) was clearly designed by Marot, by reference particularly to his Treveszaal in the Binnenhof Palace in The Hague. Its vigorous woodcarving by John Selden, who was also a decorative sculptor, includes the duke's flamboyant armorials, heraldic supporters, and

Carvings between the Closterman portraits of the 6th Duke and Duchess of Somerset, including the ducal badge of KG and 'Grecian' urns, *c.*1692, by Grinling Gibbons (1648–1721)

The Carved Room showing Grinling Gibbons's carvings around two early 17th-century full-length portraits and with two of Turner's four landscapes (the nearest is *The Lake in Petworth Park* or *The Lake, Petworth: Sunset, a Stag drinking*, *c*.1828–9) painted specially for the room, and reinstated in 2002

the insignia of KG, above the two chimneypieces.

In the medieval Chapel, the duke constructed a family pew at the rear raised up above the body of the Chapel proper, which he further aggrandised by the replacement of the earlier woodwork. In 1685, Peter Voller was paid for the '63 Ballasters … inclosing [the] Communion Table' [as well as '2 Chests of Drawers for Nursery'][218] and in 1689, Isaac Greene received £5 10s for 'ye Pulpitt in ye Chappell'.[219] The Baroque pews supporting urns retain the duke's gilding and walnut graining which was applied by George Turnour in 1692.[220] Above the family pew is a conceit worthy of Versailles or Baroque Rome and a triumph of virtuoso carving. Two 'life-size' winged angels, supporting the ducal armorials, Garter and coronet, flutter in front of a deeply fringed crimson festoon curtain, looped back with simulated ropes, ribbons and tassels to reveal the opening of the family pew as if it were a theatrical box. This 'curtain' retains its original crimson and gold decoration, which originally matched the crimson velvet cushions of the '10 Chairs' and stools within the family pew.

The masterpiece of Grinling Gibbons, the famous Carved Room, is the most remarkable achievement of this period, when the duke and duchess's patronage was at its most extravagant. In 2001–2, the Carved Room was restored to its appearance in the early 19th century, when the 3rd Earl of Egremont, having doubled its size in 1793–4, created a veritable museum of 17th-century carving, amalgamating much of Selden's work with that of Gibbons. He also commissioned Jonathan Ritson (*c*.1780–1846) to provide additional carving in Gibbons style, including picture frames for four of Turner's most beautiful landscapes. Today, therefore, the Carved Room is very different to the room commissioned by the Proud Duke, but all the elements of that original room are present in the larger 'Long Dining Room', as it was often called in the 3rd Earl's day.[221]

The Carved Room represents the zenith of Gibbons's genius. It is exceptional for being a whole room in which *finesse* is unremitting. At Hampton Court the carving is intentionally more lumpen so that it could be appreciated from a distance in the immensely large state rooms. By contrast, the Carved Room repays the closest study and is awe-inspiring. In 1749 Horace Walpole enthused: 'There is one room gloriously flounced all round whole-length pictures with much the finest carving of Gibbins that ever my eyes beheld.'[222] To Walpole it was the 'most superb monument of his skill'.[223]

From at least 1743 the first room seen by tourists was the original Carved Room, then half its present size, which stood within an enfilade of rooms leading north and south, lit – as today – by west-facing windows. It was, as Walpole said, designed around full-length portraits, which were lit from the side by two (rather than four) windows. Van Dyck's unfinished *Charles I on Horseback*, now at the north end of the room, was over the sole chimneypiece, which was then opposite the windows. Visitors proceeding north up the enfilade were faced with two full-length paintings by John Closterman (*c*.1660–1711) of the *6th Duke of Somerset* (1692; no.129) and of his wife and eldest son, *Elizabeth Percy, Duchess of Somerset and the Earl of Hertford* (*c*.1692; no.127). Closterman was paid £80 for the duke's portrait in the same year (1692) that Gibbons was paid £150 for 'carveing',[224] and the magnificent double 'picture frame' which embraces Closterman's two full-lengths was specially designed for the Carved Room: it is a unique conceit in Gibbons's *oeuvre*. A second pair of whole-length portraits, now on the right-hand side of the present chimneypiece, was provided with surrounds of only slightly lesser grandeur. The picture frames are lightness personified, again the only example of their kind in Gibbons's output to be hollowed out in this way, with acanthus scrolls and ornament intricately carved around and within a hollow centre. These superb *tours de force* of carving were meant to be seen in a sidelight, instead of *contre-jour* as they are now, and this would have emphasised their sculptural volume, or rather their lightness and lack of volume. Some of the imagery obviously refers to the duke and duchess (the armorials, the insignia of the Garter, ciphers and coronets for example), and it is likely that the remainder was intended to suggest their interests in music, collecting and horticulture.

Concurrently, the Somersets were commissioning and collecting on a royal scale. Indeed, the duchess was a close friend of Queen

Cabinet on stand, detail of inside drawer-fronts *[below]*, **detail of doors** *[above]*, **Japan, *c*.1690–1700.**
Lacquer, mounted in gilt bronze, 114 x 105 x 54 cm. (Grand Staircase)

Mary II. Both ladies were smitten with fashionable china-mania, which swept through the Northern European courts when imports from the Far East were increasing in volume. This explains the presence of a rare series of carved walnut stands, *c.*1690, of three different designs, as supports for massive blue-and-white 17th-century Chinese lidded jars. According to the 1750 inventory, vases on stands were placed in several prominent rooms, including the King of Spain's Bedchamber, either as singletons or pairs.

Lacquer too was immensely popular in the Somersets' aristocratic milieu. Petworth retains such things as a small *namban* (Japanese export) domed-topped coffer, *c.*1620–40 (Mrs Wyndham's Bedroom; Lord Egremont Collection), and several Chinese or Japanese lacquer cabinets and coffers, *c.*1690–1700, some of which were given splendid giltwood carved cabriole-legged stands in the 18th century. They were widely distributed about the house in 1750, mainly in the grandest bedrooms. The giltwood stand, *c.*1755, of the lacquer cabinet (Mrs Wyndham's Bedroom) was probably made by James and Thomas Whittle, exhibiting their typical fluidity of design and carving. They were not the sole suppliers of such things to the 2nd Earl of Egremont. One extravagant stand for a Chinese cabinet was made in 1758 by Thomas Watts and was 'inrichd with Foliage Bands, Shell work and Mosake grounds'.[225] The fashion for Oriental black and gold lacquer clearly influenced the duke in his purchase of a set of five Florentine five-legged tables, *c.*1700 (the fifth central leg being designed to support the weight of sculpture, thus avoiding the risk of cracking the marble table top). They have all been redecorated in the 19th century, apart from the one in the Grand Staircase, set against a niche containing Honoré Pelle's Bernini-esque bust of *James II*. The table in this set on the pier of the Little Dining has an Italian Jasper marble top, which is probably one of two supplied by Grinling Gibbons in 1695.[226]

Many pieces of fine furniture survive from the Somersets' reign, including a French or Anglo-French 'Boulle' table and flanking stands, *c.*1685 (Lord Egremont Collection), which stood in the King of Spain's Bedchamber in 1750; pier-glasses with *verre églomisé* and 'seaweed' marquetry pieces (Lord Egremont Collection), the latter probably by Gerrit Jensen (active 1677–d.1715), who charged the duchess £119 15s for furniture in 1692.[227] Equally, much furniture described in the 1750 inventory has disappeared, including the silver-embroidered green-and-white satin state bed provided for the King of Spain's Bedchamber (now the White Library) before 1703. In April 1756 'Carr the Mercer' (presumably Robert Carr, who supplied textiles for use at George III's coronation in 1760) was paid £344 for 'crimson damask for the King of Spain's apartment'.[228] The white-and-gold-framed state bed hung with

crimson silk damask, *c.*1758 (Lord Egremont Collection; Mrs Wyndham's Bedroom) – whose dome is surmounted by a squirrel climbing a tree, apparently inspired by the designs of Thomas Johnson – is one of the masterpieces of the English Rococo.[229] Its maker is unknown, but it was presumably supplied by the London firm of Whittle & Norman, chief suppliers to the 2nd Earl. The crimson damask would also have covered the chairs, some of which survive, and the curtains *en suite*.

The bed originally stood in the ground-floor State Bedroom. Next door was then the King of Spain's Drawing Room (the present White and Gold Room, so-called because of its décor, which incorporates Rococo carved wall panels). Five drawings of the room, *c.*1840, within a portfolio embossed with the title 'Drawings by Jonathan Ritson', may suggest that the White and Gold Room was designed in neo-Rococo style by Ritson, but this seems unlikely, given that Ritson's known carvings at Petworth are solely in the Carved Room, in a coarser version of Gibbons's style.[230] Also, the drawings seem to be of an existing interior rather than designs for new carving and panelling. There may have been later alterations in the White and Gold Room: the corners of the carved dado panels may be additions of *c.*1840. But the room as a whole seems entirely in keeping with the style of the carvers employed by the 2nd Earl, who were presumably working to designs supplied via Matthew Brettingham the Elder, the supervising architect, who may have designed the White and Gold Room himself. The major payments in the 2nd Earl's accounts at this time were to English craftsmen, so the White and Gold Room, which has been described as 'one of the purest Louis XV interiors in England', was presumably no exception.[231] Indeed, the Rococo carving is analogous to the series of pier-glasses and other carved and gilded furniture attributed to James Whittle and Samuel Norman. Another drawing in the Petworth Archives, annotated 'Supposed Door for Petworth' in a later hand (probably that of Thomas Sockett, the 3rd Earl's chaplain and factotum), depicts one wall of a similar, though more elaborate, Rococo room. This has much more of the feel of a design and could well date from around 1760, so may have been a *première pensée*.[232]

State bed, attributed to James Whittle and Samuel Norman, *c.*1758. Gilded and painted wood, and partly original and partly modern, crimson damask and *passementerie*, 276 cm high. (Mrs Wyndham's Bedroom; Lord Egremont Collection)

Comparison of the 1750 inventory with the 2nd Earl of Egremont's posthumous inventory of 1764 reveals that the 2nd Earl transformed Petworth, while retaining much that had gone before, as indeed did his son, the 3rd Earl, who ruled at Petworth until 1837. In 1750, the 2nd Earl paid the huge sum of £912 for furniture from the 7th Duke's personal estate.[233] Indeed, several pieces ordered by the 6th Duke in the 1730s, including elegant carved giltwood side- and pier-tables in an Italianate Kentian style, are quite in keeping with the 2nd Earl's own taste. Two carved giltwood tables, *c.*1735–40 (Carved Room), may have had their Roman *verde antico* tops, bordered with porphyry and mounted in gilt bronze, added by the 2nd Earl. The similar pier-table, *c.*1735–40, in the Beauty Room, was brought up to date by Samuel Norman in 1760 and 1762 by decorative additions, including the Rococo pendant carving in the centre of the frieze. This is a classic example of 18th-century economy in the preservation and use of existing high-quality materials.[234]

In the Square Dining Room is a set of five carved and painted serving tables which was probably inaugurated by the Proud Duke, given that the pair flanking the chimneypiece may be the '2 Marble Side board Tables' listed in the 6th Duke's Dining Room (the present Beauty Room) in 1750.[235] The 1764 inventory describes the 'large Side-Board Table' opposite as 'Carv'd & Painted white to Match the other two', so it must have been added between 1750 and 1763 by the 2nd Earl. The pair of matching tables either side of the Marble Hall door was not listed in 1764, but was there in 1837 and so must have been commissioned by the 3rd Earl: one of them is depicted in Turner's watercolour/gouache view (1827) of the room. This gradual accretion of a set of tables in the Square Dining Room indicates both conservatism and pragmatism in the tastes of three successive owners of Petworth.[236] In his view of the Square Dining Room, Turner also depicts a carved giltwood pier-glass and table, *c.*1755, one of a pair attributed to James and Thomas Whittle.

Pier-glass (detail) by James Whittle and Samuel Norman (*c.*1754–9). Giltwood, 426 cm high; **and pier-table, Italian, *c.*1730.** Giltwood with shaped white marble top, 85.5 x 187.5 x 75 cm. (Red Room). **The largest and most elaborate of a series of glasses supplied to the 2nd Earl by Whittle and Norman**

The 2nd Earl and Countess of Egremont (who was closely involved) employed a host of London craftsmen for Petworth and Egremont House, their London residence in Piccadilly, which was built in Palladian style by Matthew Brettingham (1699–1769).[237] They included James Whittle (active 1731–d.1759), who was in partnership first with his son, Thomas (d.1755) and then with his son-in-law and partner, Samuel Norman (active 1746–67), and Norman's close associate Paul Saunders (1722–71), Tapestry Maker to George III. The furniture in both houses was amalgamated in 1794, when Egremont House was sold by the 3rd Earl, who sent most of the pictures to

Pier-glass (detail) by James Whittle and Samuel Norman (*c.*1754–9)

auction, but retained much of the furniture. The series of Rococo carved giltwood pier-glasses, *c.*1754–59, is one of the glories of Petworth. They are attributed to James and Thomas Whittle and Samuel Norman because the 2nd Earl is known to have been a major customer of theirs (particularly for Egremont House) and also on the basis of similar documented furniture at Holkham Hall, Norfolk and Woburn Abbey, Bedfordshire. The pier-glass in the Somerset Room is very similar to a pair of glasses at Holkham ascribed to James Whittle by his near-contemporary, Matthew Brettingham the Younger.[238] There were considerable payments in 1754–9 to James and Thomas Whittle and then Whittle & Norman, presumably partly connected to these pier-glasses. Most of the payments to the firm appear in the 2nd Earl's bank account at Drummond's.[239]

Whittle & Norman's most magnificent pier-glass (Red Room) is a colossal *tour de force* of naturalistic Rococo woodcarving, incorporating three cranes with necks and wings outstretched at the apex of a riot of sinuous branches, garlands and scrolls. The design seems to derive from a design by Lock and Copeland.[240] The overmantel glass (Square Dining Room) was supplied by James Whittle and Samuel Norman for the same position in the State Bedroom (now the White Library). Other superbly carved giltwood furniture includes a set of four torchère stands, *c.*1763 (Lord Egremont) by Samuel Norman, who was paid £75 12s in 1763, when he supplied them for the Tapestry Room at Egremont House.[241] Numerous sets of such stands were listed at both Egremont House and Petworth in 1764. In 1753 Whittle was paid 'in full for Gilt

Frames', so the firm also supplied frames for the earl's pictures.[242]

Furniture was often re-covered or modified for use at Egremont House. This was partly to save money, but also to make existing furniture more fashionable and more in keeping with carefully considered arrangements and symmetrical picture hangs in rooms where even the picture ropes matched the mainly crimson and blue wall-hangings and curtains. In its brief heyday, Egremont House was one of the most sophisticated ensembles in the capital, the rooms of parade on the first floor being arranged – as at Brettingham's Norfolk House, St James's Square – around the staircase to create a circuit for guests on gala evenings. Following his disastrous warehouse fire in 1759, when he was already probably engaged for Egremont House, and subsequently between 1760 and 1764, Norman charged the huge sum of £2,519 10s 6d and was paid about £1,700 for various works, including the provision, alteration, embellishment, covering or re-covering of furniture, and for making up damask curtains and wall-hangings, hanging pictures and gilding seven rooms.

Samuel Norman probably beautified, as was his practice with other side tables for Egremont House, the front aprons of the pair of giltwood Roman console tables supporting shaped black-and-white marble tops with gilt-bronze mounts, *c.*1760 (Carved Room). These tables are presumably the *bianco e nero* tables obtained in 1760 from 'Mr. Wilton', probably the sculptor, Joseph Wilton, RA (1722–1803).[243] The striated *bianco e nero antico* marble is originally French, from the quarry of Aubert in the Pyrenees, which was probably mined there by the Romans from the 4th century AD. Indeed, the tops may well be made up of marble quarried in Antiquity.[244] The gilt-bronze mounts framing the marble suggest Roman manufacture. This pair of tables is distinctive for a 'sword drawer' (probably designed for maps and rolled documents rather than weapons) at the back running horizontally across the full width (not an English characteristic).[245] They stand on the end piers of the Carved Room, where they were depicted in C.R. Leslie's oil painting of *c.*1828 (Tate Britain).

Egremont was a pioneering collector of French furniture.[246] In 1741, he paid Lord Denbigh (the 5th Earl) £33 3s 6d for 'tapestry fauteuils [armchairs] from Paris';[247] in 1752 he bought at Prestage's auction rooms a 'French Commode, £21. 6. 0';[248] and in 1761–3 he paid out £230 to 'L. Beauvais', which suggests a connection with the French tapestry manufactory there.[249] In 1763 two red Boulle desks were inventoried in bedrooms, in use as dressing tables, which are presumably the *bureau Mazarin*, *c.*1700–10, and the *bureau-brisé*, *c.*1680 (both Somerset Room).[250] These are early references to antique French furniture in an English collection. The *bureau Mazarin* is of the same model as the desk in the Swedish Royal Collection, Stockholm, which bears the stamp of

Nicolas Sageot (1666–1731; *maître* 1706), although the latter top is of a different design. Sageot is known to have used Toussaint Devoye (active *c.*1706–48) as a marquetry cutter, to whom the Petworth desk-top is attributed. The overall style is inspired by the fanciful designs of Jean Berain (1640–1711).

The other desk is earlier, *c.*1680, and is of the type called a *bureau-brisé*, in other words, a desk with an opening top (one half folds back to reveal the interior). Although it is of very high quality, it cannot be attributed to any single maker. It is stamped by Charles-Michel Cochois (*maître* before 1737, d. 1764) and bears the crowned 'C' mark for 1745–9 on the top gilt-bronze mount on the left-hand leg. Cochois was also a dealer, which presumably explains the mark, though he may also have repaired the desk. Egremont may also have been responsible for acquiring a large red Boulle cupboard *c.*1720 (Bedroom Corridor; Lord Egremont Collection) in the style of Nicolas Sageot.

***Bureau-brisé*: Paris, *c.*1680.** Boulle marquetry of red tortoiseshell, brass, and pewter; the interior of red tortoiseshell inlaid with ivory, 86 x 120 x 71 cm. **This writing desk was probably acquired by the 2nd Earl of Egremont, and was probably one of two listed at Petworth in 1763 (Somerset Room)**

Given that the 3rd Earl of Egremont's entertaining at Petworth involved maintaining 'open house' in medieval fashion, much new practical furniture was required, such as dining chairs, tables and so on. Mahogany furniture of this kind was supplied in 1787–1802 by John Kerr of 31 Pall Mall, London. The dining chairs, with crimson leather seats (Square Dining Room) may derive from the '24 Strong Plain Mahog. Chairs with Broad Tablets in backs' supplied by Kerr for £33 in 1802.[251] The top of the vast mahogany dining table originally made for the Carved Room (*c.*1830; Lord Egremont Collection) is inlaid with *pietre dure*.

The 3rd Earl also gave a large commission to Thomas Chippendale in 1777–8.[252] The most outstanding things are three large state beds, each costing about £90 for the bedstock, canopy and fittings, the silk lining, lace and fringe (one on show in the Belzamine Bedroom, Lord Egremont Collection). Chippendale also supplied the mattresses, quilts and blankets, while Lord Egremont provided the 'rich floured velvet' bought for £469 from the Spitalfields weavers Charles Triquet and John van Sommer as early as 1764. There is also seat furniture incorporating a partitioned giltwood sofa and 12 matching armchairs (the sofa and part of the set is in the Somerset Room; Lord Egremont Collection and NT). The sofa, with its separate elbow partitions at either end, is unique in Chippendale's *oeuvre* and is probably linked to the 3rd Earl's large payment to his firm of £959 10s on 12

August 1778. Strangely enough, a sofa with 'Ealbow Partitions' was listed in the State Bedroom at Petworth in 1763, but it cannot have been this one, which is stylistically typical of the late 1770s. Reminiscent of Chippendale's earlier style are the four painted stools in the Marble Hall. These have dished seats and distinctive sinuous supports. They may be from a set of eight listed here in 1764: 'Eight Hall Stools with Coat of Arms painted on the Seat'. If so, they were probably repainted when the 2nd Lord Leconfield decorated the room, *c.*1869–72, during Salvin's works at Petworth. They are similar in shape to the 26 mahogany stools supplied by Chippendale in 1764 to the Library at Christ Church, Oxford.[253] However, there is no mention of Chippendale in the 2nd Earl's accounts.

Like his father, the 3rd Earl also bought French furniture, beginning with 'une pendule doré d'ormoullu' for 1,080 *livres* in 1774–5, which he bought from Marc Sayde, a Parisian *marchand-mercier*, while he was on his Grand Tour.[254] From 1 to 28 July 1802, with many other English tourists, he was in Paris during the Peace of Amiens, when he probably bought from the fashionable shop of Martin-Eloi Lignereux a pair of gilt-bronze candelabra, supported by patinated bronze figures of *Egyptiennes* (White and Gold Room; Lord Egremont Collection), which are identical to a pair at Uppark (NT) and in the Royal Collection. The latter two pairs were bought by Egremont's friend, Sir Harry Fetherstonhaugh, 2nd Bt, who was one of the Prince Regent's artistic advisers, so the 3rd Earl's purchase was in the vanguard of fashion.[255] Lignereux's partner, Dominique Daguerre, was closely involved in the prince's Carlton House and was influential in promulgating French taste in London.

In 1807 the 3rd Earl purchased for £19 the roll-top desk, Paris, *c.*1780 (White and Gold Room; Lord Egremont Collection), stamped by François Rübestück (*c.*1722–85; *maître* 1766).[256] This masculine and practical piece of furniture, veneered with red *satiné* and purplewood with gilt-bronze mounts and Greek key bandings indicative of early French Neo-classicism, would have still been agreeably modern-looking

[left]
Pair of five-light candelabra, Paris, probably supplied by M.-E. Lignereux in 1802. *Verde antico* marble, patinated and gilt bronze. 60 cm high (to top of figure); 82 cm high (overall), (White and Gold Room; Lord Egremont Collection)

to an English collector in 1807. It bears the initials 'LD' under a count's coronet for an as yet unidentified French nobleman.[257]

On the central window pier of the Carved Room stands a French carved giltwood side-table, *c.*1700, bearing the cross of Lorraine as part of the decoration of its frieze and baluster-shaped legs. This table is first recorded at Petworth in Leslie's *Carved Room*, *c.*1828.[258] It does not figure in the posthumous inventories of the 2nd Earl, so it must have been acquired by the 3rd Earl, who gave it a place of honour in the Carved Room. It has now been returned to the central pier as shown by Leslie. The solid porphyry top is not original, and must have been added in the early 19th century. The general design is close to a table with fleur-de-lis armorials at Versailles;[259] another in a Parisian private collection bearing the arms, in the central frieze cartouche, of Président Molé de Champlâtreux; and a table in the Louvre (OA 5049), which was made in 1713 for Charles-Henri II de Malon de Bercy (1678–1742), Surintendant des Finances, for the château de Bercy, east of Paris. The carved work at Bercy, some of which survives, was done by *sculpteurs* of the *Bâtiments du Roi*, whose craftsmen developed the *Régence* style.[260] The Louvre table – with the arms of its patron hacked away from the central frieze *cartouche* – is stylistically *retardataire*, being still related to similar tables of *c.*1690–1710, but with *Régence* elements. These tables are also related to a design (*c.*1680–90; Paris, École Nationale Supérieure des Beaux-Arts) by the sculptor Christophe Charmeton (1655–1708) for a table decorated with the royal fleurs-de-lis. Such tables

[below]
Side-table, decorated with the Cross of Lorraine, French, *c.*1700, with a later porphyry top (*c.*1810?), carved and gilded pine, 87.4 x 161.3 x 83.7 cm (Carved Room)

were often used for the display of bronzes or other works of art. The central cartouches in the frieze are reminiscent of those depicted in Pierre Lepautre's *Livre de tables qui sont dans les appartements du Roy sur lesquels sont posés les bijoux du Cabinet des médailles* ['Book of tables in the King's Apartments on which are placed the jewels from the Medal Cabinet'], *c.*1700. Lepautre's book of designs also includes similar tables with elaborately carved legs joined by undulating stretchers.[261]

Like the Bercy table in the Louvre, the central cartouche in the frieze of the Petworth table is blank, but may once have borne the arms of the table's patron, presumably a member of the house of Lorraine. The cross of Lorraine recalls the title 'King of Jerusalem', which the dukes of Lorraine bore via King René of Anjou (1409–80). The most likely candidate as commissioner of the table is duc Léopold I de Lorraine et de Bar (1679–1729; succ. 1697). The décor (*c.*1719) of his bedroom at the château of Lunéville, Meurthe-et-Moselle, designed by Germain Boffrand, also incorporates the cross of Lorraine. The posthumous sale (1781) in Brussels of the effects of his son, prince Charles-Alexandre-Emmanuel de Lorraine, duc de Lorraine et de Bar,

[below]
Sarcophagus-shaped commode, by André-Charles Boulle (1642–1732) and workshop, *c.*1710. Veneered with marquetry of brass and tortoiseshell, 86.8 x 125.6 x 62.3 cm. **Acquired by the 2nd Lord Leconfield in 1882. A pair of commodes, of the same model, was supplied by Boulle to Louis XIV in 1708 (the sole documented surviving furniture by Boulle himself).** (Red Room)

[right]
Detail of the above

may have been the moment when the Petworth table entered the market. Furniture with a Lorraine provenance is recorded in late 18th- and early 19th-century London auctions.[262]

The giltwood pier-table in the Somerset Room was stamped by Jean-Baptiste-Claude Sené (1748–1803; *maître* 1769), a *menuisier* of distinction, who was appointed *fournisseur de la Couronne* in 1785. His glittering clientele included Marie-Antoinette, whose monumental bed at Fontainebleau (1787) was the product of Sené's collaboration with other royal craftsmen under the direction of the *sculpteur* Hauré. The records of the royal *Garde-Meuble* and the *Menus-Plaisirs* indicate that Sené made beds, chairs, tables and consoles for St Cloud which were decorated with emblems appropriate to both Louis XVI and Marie-Antoinette.[263] The stretcher of the Petworth table is in the form of Apollo's lyre, which Sené also employed for backs of chairs. The half-moon shape, the Neo-classical ornament and the red *griotte* marble top are all typical of the developed Louis XVI style. The provenance of the table is unknown, as is the date of its entry into the Egremont collection, but it may well be an acquisition of the Francophile 3rd Earl.

The last distinguished moment for the Petworth furniture collection was the purchase by the 2nd Lord Leconfield from Colnaghi's, the eminent London dealer, of a tranche of French furniture, bought at the legendary Hamilton Palace sale at Christie's, which consisted of 2,213 lots sold in London, 17 June–20 July 1882. Lord Leconfield's acquisitions were a commode, a *bureau plat,* two clocks (all of Boulle marquetry), four giltwood armchairs covered in Beauvais tapestry (White and Gold Room; Lord Egremont Collection), and a majestic lacquer screen. The star ex-Hamilton piece at Petworth is the National Trust's finest example of Boulle furniture: a near-contemporaneous version (*c.*1710) of Boulle's Grand Trianon pair of sarcophagus-shaped commodes supplied to Louis XIV by Boulle in 1708. They were intended for the King's Bedroom at the Grand Trianon in the park at Versailles, but are now within the palace itself.[264] The pair of Trianon commodes is the sole furniture documented as by Boulle and as such is fundamental to the consideration of his *oeuvre,* as is the Petworth version of the model (Red Room). Like the Versailles pair, it was made in Boulle's workshop in the Louvre, Paris, and is identical with only minor variations.[265] The sarcophagus shape represents a transitional stage in furniture design between the side- or console table and the chest of drawers, deriving from Boulle's experiments with new furniture shapes and functions. When the Versailles pair was made, 'commode' as a noun meaning a 'chest of drawers' did not exist (as an adjective, it means 'convenient'). Thus Boulle was paid 3,000 *livres* in 1708 for 'deux bureaux [tables] qu'il fait pour le palais de Trianon.'[266] The gilt-bronze mounts are sculptural, being distinctive for the corner mounts in the form of winged sphinxes with lions' feet, as they were described in the Trianon inventory of 1718: 'aux coins sont quatre sphinx ailés aussi de bronze doré, terminés d'une patte de lion avec feuillages'.[267] Despite the royal commission – which might have implied a unique design for the king – Boulle made several versions of his celebrated Trianon model for other clients, and the sphinx corner mounts, shorn of their wings, also appear in writing tables (*bureaux plats*) supplied by his workshop.[268] This concept of legs ornamented with kingly imagery (such as sphinxes and lions) derives from antique Roman furniture, and in particular from Roman thrones.[269] The plate photograph in the 1882 sale catalogue indicates that the commode's beautifully modelled, chased and gilded mounts were then much cleaner and more refulgent (they still retain most of their original gilding).

During the 1853 Gore House exhibition in London to which it was lent by the 12th Duke of Hamilton,[270] the Hamilton Palace (Petworth) commode was copied for the 4th Marquess of Hertford (1800–70), the Paris-based principal creator of the Wallace Collection. Despite his knowledge of French collections, Hertford must either have been unaware of the original pair made for Louis XIV, which had been moved after the Revolution (in 1790) from Versailles to the Bibliothèque Mazarine, Paris, or – if he did know of them – had failed to obtain permission to have them copied. His commission of a pair of copies may suggest the latter. However, there is no mention of the Versailles/Mazarine commodes in Lord Hertford's correspondence. The copies made for Hertford in London are almost certainly those in the Frick Collection, New York.[271] They are highly accurate, with very minor variations, and of high quality. They were made via the intervention of Edward Rutter, a Paris-based English dealer, by John Webb, dealer and cabinetmaker of 22 Cork Street, London, who made other copies of fine French furniture for Hertford. The copies are specified in Webb's bill (under December 1855) and cost £650 for the pair.[272] The very high-quality gilt-bronze mounts are stamped 'Blake' and 'Blake. London', for the London firm of cabinetmakers of that name, which was presumably subcontracted by Webb.

The Petworth commode is further linked to the Frick Collection pair by the identical marble tops of all three, which are thinner and differently shaped by comparison to the two Versailles commodes, the latter retaining Boulle's thicker, more robustly moulded, tops of red *griotte* marble. When the Petworth commode was lent to the Gore House exhibition in 1853, the catalogue photograph reveals that it had a different top to the one it has now (which was in place by the time of the photograph of the commode in the 1882 Hamilton Palace sale catalogue). The new top must, therefore, have been fitted between 1853 and 1882. The previous marble top of the Petworth commode, photographed in 1853, was clearly not the original, and was too large, greatly overlapping the sides.

Although there are other early 18th-century versions of this model of Boulle commode (e.g. at Vaux-le-Vicomte and in the Metropolitan Museum of Art, New York),[273] the Petworth example takes pride of place after the Versailles originals because the Petworth commode – via the Frick copies – is the *fons et origo* of all post-1853 versions.[274] It is also in good condition, untouched by radical restoration.

What of the other Hamilton Palace furniture which was translated to Petworth after the 1882 sale? The large elaborately mounted *bureau plat* (Red Room) was purchased for £315: '526 AN OBLONG WRITING-TABLE, by Buhl, mounted with terminal figures, masks, and ornaments of ormolu – 76in. long by 38 in. wide.' Until recently, it was thought to be attributable to Boulle's workshop, but it is clearly a very good and very grand mid-19th-century example in the manner of Boulle. The wasp-waisted top is untypical of pieces from Boulle's workshop, the mounts have a distinctly 19th-century feel and the condition of the interior is too clean to have been made in the early 18th century.

The larger of the two clocks is the sole piece in red Boulle marquetry (Square Dining Room). The movement is signed by Nicolas Delaunay (d. before 1738) and, like the case, is *c.*1715. It was lot 661 in

***Bureau plat* (writing table), Paris, *c.*1850.** Veneered with marquetry of brass and tortoiseshell, 80 x 193.8 x 97.2 cm. Acquired by the 2nd Lord Leconfield in 1882. (Red Room)

Bureau plat (writing table), *c.*1850. Detail of gilt bronze head (a river god?) flanking the kneehole of the desk

the Hamilton Palace sale and fetched £367 10s: 'A LOUIS XIV. CLOCK, with enamelled dial, chased with medallion of the king and crown, in case of red buhl, surmounted by a figure of Fame, with Apollo in his car and other figures in ormolu, and feet formed of horses on red buhl plinth.'[275] Another smaller black Boulle marquetry clock (Carved Room) is signed 'Minoche à Paris' for either Nicolas (*maître* 1684; d. after 1740) or Jean (*maître* 1693; d. after 1740) Minoche. It was lot 1787 and was bought for £52 10s. It is similar to a clock at Boughton House, Northamptonshire.[276]

Lord Leconfield also bought for £315 four giltwood armchairs covered in floral Beauvais tapestry (White and Gold Room; Lord Egremont Collection) from a set of twelve: '1913 A SET OF FOUR LOUIS XIV. CARVED AND GILT FAUTEUILS, covered in old Gobelins tapestry, with baskets of flowers'. These chairs are not stamped and date from *c.*1760. With their flowing Rococo lines, these are just the sort of chairs that inspired the 2nd Earl of Egremont's cabinetmaker and upholsterer, Samuel Norman and Paul Saunders, in the design of seat furniture for Egremont House in the early 1760s. They are certainly the chairs bought at the Hamilton Palace sale via Colnaghi, as photographs were taken for the 1882 sale catalogue, and they also appear in a pre-1882 photograph of the Palace's Sitting Room.

[above]
Clock with movement by Nicolas Delaunay (died before 1738), *c*.1715. Acquired by the 2nd Lord Leconfield after the 1882 Hamilton Palace sale. Mounted in gilt bronze and veneered with marquetry of brass and red tortoiseshell, 67 x 43 x 25 cm. (Square Dining Room)

[right]
Armchair (one of four), Paris, *c*.1760. Carved and gilt wood, upholstered, with Beauvais tapestry covers, 111 x 73 x 83 cm. **Acquired by the 2nd Lord Leconfield in 1882.** (Lord Egremont Collection; White and Gold Room)

The final piece of furniture acquired by Lord Leconfield in the 1882 sale is of a different character altogether. It is a huge six-fold lacquer screen bearing the arms of the Dukes of Hamilton. It was clearly an export commission made in China in the late 17th century. Given the presence of the ducal arms, it was probably ordered from China by the 4th Duke of Hamilton (1658–1712), who was Ambassador to Louis XIV, Master of the Great Wardrobe and a great collector. It was lot 649 in the 1882 sale and was acquired for £220 10s by Colnaghi.

The 2nd Lord Leconfield was an expert on agriculture and was certainly not a collector *per se*. His interest in furniture was presumably mainly due (like his extensive patronage at Petworth) to his wife, Lady Constance Primrose, a member of the artistic/intellectual aristocratic *côterie* known as 'The Souls'.[277] She was the younger sister of the 5th Earl of Rosebery (the Prime Minister), who inherited in 1878 the rich collection of French furniture at Mentmore, Buckinghamshire, through his wife, Hannah de Rothschild.[278]

Lord Leconfield and his wife, Constance, were patrons of Anthony Salvin (who undertook the remodelling of the Carved Room) and of William Morris, by whom there are chairs covered in rare printed velvet by the Morris factory (Mrs Wyndham's Dressing Room). Morris's commission at Petworth to supply wallpapers, wall-hangings, curtains, druggets, light fittings and furniture is a rare example of his firm addressing the needs of a major country house. The Leconfields found Morris exasperating. In *Random Papers*, Lady Leconfield remembered that commissioning the silk of 'Larkspur' pattern for the Carved and Red rooms caused immense difficulty owing to Morris's stubbornness and intransigence. The result of this commission is recorded in early *Country Life* photographs, while the silk of the Red Room curtains still survives in situ (albeit converted to festoons in the 19th century).

9

The park, pleasure ground and estate

Petworth park is hallowed for its inspiration of Turner, whose landscapes – painted *c.*1828–30 for the 3rd Earl of Egremont and set into the panelling of the Carved Room – are radiant with the colours of sunset. It is still possible to look through the tall windows from Turner's landscape paintings and identify the same scenes outside. After the great storms of 1987 and 1989, some 32,000 trees have been planted, following study of the wreckage and extensive archival research. The park beloved of Turner was the creation of Lancelot 'Capability' Brown, whose employment by the 2nd Earl of Egremont, between 1751 and 1765, transformed the formality of the earlier layout, designed for the 6th Duke of Somerset by the royal gardener, George London,

The west front from the lake, with the Petworth church tower just visible behind the house (Barry's 1827 spire was taken down in the mid-20th century)

[left]
***Petworth, Sussex, the Seat of the Earl of Egremont: Dewy Morning*, by J.M.W. Turner (1775–1851), exhibited 1810.** Oil on canvas, 91.5 x 120.5 cm. (Tate)

The north end of the west front seen through the iron screen, based on Tijou's designs for Hampton Court, and erected by the 2nd Lord Leconfield, *c.*1869–72

[right]
The ha-ha protecting the wooded Pleasure Ground to the north of the west front

around 1700. The history of Petworth park is, however, much more ancient, reaching back into the Middle Ages, as Horace Walpole realised when he described it as 'Percy to the backbone'.[279]

William, 8th Baron de Percy (1193–1245), had a 'new small park in which is his *cunegaria* [rabbit warren]'. In 1499 the 5th Earl of Northumberland added 105 acres, and in the course of the 16th century more common land was enclosed until, by 1621, the park was about 400 acres (it is now 700 acres). In 1574 the 8th Earl of Northumberland's surveyors noted two main parks ('Greate' and 'Lyttyl'), both of which were scantily planted with oak and beech. The little park, to the north-west of the house, was about 220 acres and contained '72 deare'. Its central feature, still known as Arbour Hill, had 'divers pleasant walks'. From this vantage point, it was possible to view the progress of stag-hunting in the valley beneath. Henry VIII erected a banqueting house here when Petworth became crown property on the death of the 6th Earl of Northumberland in 1537.

The Percys' fortified manor house was enclosed by walled gardens which, in 1327, contained 'certain ponds'. The bird's-eye views of Ralph Treswell (1610) and John Norden (1625) show, within new walks, the parterre and fountain installed by the 8th Earl during his extensive improvements of 1576–82. In 1610, to the west, was a rose garden, with a bowling green, orchard, fishpond and vegetable garden beyond. The 8th Earl (who was to die miserably in the Tower) also laid out 'new walkes' to the north of the house, and these, also known as the birch or 'birchen' walks, were later incorporated into the Pleasure Ground. Like his father, the scholarly 9th, or 'Wizard', Earl was a keen gardener, as his library proves. Among several horticultural works was *The Gardeners Labyrinth*, an early treatise of 1579. However, despite the grandiose plans for Petworth conceived during his long imprisonment in the Tower following the Gunpowder Plot, and the 'glorious leisure' that he enjoyed at Petworth from 1621, he seems to have left his father's arrangements largely intact, apart from the construction of the huge quadrangular stables and riding school shown to the west of the house in Norden's map. By 1635 the hill running east to west from the north end of the house to the lake was terraced in 'rampires' or ramparts, and this work was continued by the 10th Earl (prominent courtier, High Admiral, friend and then opponent of Charles I, and Van Dyck's patron) in 1636. The terraces are shown in a view of *c.*1680, which also depicts the extensions to the house made by the 9th and 10th earls, the 9th Earl's stables in the foreground, and something of the gardens, all of which were described as 'so magnificent and complete' in 1635 by Lord Hammond, who saw 'walks, Gardens, Orchards, Bowling Ground, Stables and Fish-ponds' surrounding 'this Prince-like House'.

The Proud Duke wanted a grandiose setting for his new house and George London's work for William III at Hampton Court and elsewhere eminently qualified him to provide it. The gardens were proceeding apace by 1689, when London was paid 'for levelling and planting the kitchen garden'. Like the 8th, 9th and 10th earls, the duke had a real interest in gardening, which he shared with his friend William Bentinck, 1st Earl of Portland, William III's favourite and the Superintendent of the Royal Gardens. In 1699, for example, Portland offered to buy plants in Holland on the duke's behalf and he would certainly have encouraged the duke to employ London, who was both his Deputy Superintendent and Master Gardener.

A painting of after 1706 (Belvoir Castle; Duke of Rutland Collection) shows the completed west front and forecourt. To the south (on the right side of the painting) are elm walks, to the north the imposing greenhouse and to the west, the 'Vistoe from the front to Tillington',

which was planted as a lime avenue, interrupted (until its demolition between 1706 and 1722) by the 9th Earl's stables quadrangle. The map of 1706 shows the layout, and the proximity of the public road to the south of the great avenue. To the north of the avenue were three terraces, 'hewn and made out of the Rocke, of 600 foot in length' (as Hammond noted in 1635), which the duke embellished between 1689 and 1704 by realigning the steps between the terraces, and in 1692 by erecting gate-piers and 'a seat that stands in the lower rampier', which were carved by John Selden. The terraces and the rest of the gardens were symmetrically ornamented with flowers in pots and clipped trees in tubs. In 1689 'Mr Vespreetes man' (i.e. an employee of Antony Versprit, the foremost nurseryman of the day, and possibly the 'Dutch Gardner' mentioned in the ducal accounts) was paid 5s for 'presenting 2 potts of flowers', and a mason was paid for 'flower potts upon peeres by the Great Steppes'.

The Orangery stood at the north end of a rectangular walled orange garden, which covered an acre of ground stretching northwards from the chapel cloister at the north end of the house. This was called 'the new orange garden next ye chappell' in 1692, and within it the orange trees were set in painted 'oring tubs', which would have been placed in formal patterns within the parterres marked out by painted 'Border boards'. The Duke took a close interest in his orange trees, asking his gardener, Miller, in July 1703 'if the orange trees are in blossom and how much' (the flowers were used to decorate the house) and on 22 August he instructed Miller to carry them back into the Orangery for over-wintering 'and not venture them abroad any longer'. At this point, the orange trees 'in double roes on each side that walk from ye house to ye oringe house' were replaced for the winter by more hardy 'Bays and Lauristinus &c. ... in two lines in the roome of the orange trees'. Thus the symmetrical effect was maintained.

Immediately to the west of the walled orangery garden was the flower garden, dominated by a great greenhouse to the north, between the Orangery and the terraces. In front of the greenhouse was a parterre with at least two lead statues and with a central fountain served by a fountain house on the top of the terraces. The fountain house doubled as a banqueting house and was provided with a polished marble table carved by Selden in 1696 – on 29 May 1702 the duke's steward recorded that the Duke was 'at super in the Sumer house'. Vegetables were provided from the huge kitchen garden to the south of the house. This had been the site of the earlier kitchen garden (shown in the painting of *c.*1680 at Syon) and was altered and enlarged by the duke in 1689–after 1703, using bricks made in a kiln in the park. The work was supervised in its latter stages by Miller, whose son took over the general garden administration. The duke was soon 'very much

Ionic rotunda in the Pleasure Ground, *c.*1760, attributed to Matthew Brettingham the Elder (d.1769) and probably commissioned by the 2nd Earl of Egremont

dissatisfyd with his expensive management of the kitchen garden by still keeping on winter and summer 4 men and a woman when his father never had more men formerly for the kitchen garden, rampiers &c. [i.e. for the whole garden]'. His steward reported that the kitchen garden was 'in a very indifferent condition' due to blight affecting the apricots, peaches, cherries, grapes, melons and currants. Nor were there any cucumbers, 'herbs, sallatting [salad] and other things for the use of the kitchen there is soe little that if your Graces ffamily were home it would not subsist [on] them'. However, some pears, plums and 'white nutmegg peaches', 'figs and philberts' were ripe and were sent to the duke. The duke was unconvinced that this state of affairs was due to the weather (as the younger Miller had assured the steward), and Miller was sacked 'for an idle car[e]less fellow'.

Such were the duke's domestic problems in 1703, which illustrate the small labour force in a huge formal garden, and emphasise the practical as well as aesthetic purpose of horticulture in a great establishment. Petworth was (and remains) largely self-sufficient in fruit and vegetables, and the wider estate provided venison, beef, mutton, pork and fish as well as dairy products, cereals and ice. Supplies were also sent up to London, but on 1 July 1704 the duke was deprived of his usual baskets of plums and apricots by a nocturnal robber who 'came over the kitchen garden gates ... breaking one of the spikes on the top'.

Most of the 6th Duke's landscaping was obliterated in the return to 'nature' undertaken by 'Capability' Brown in the 1750s, and in the storm of 1987, but some of his sweet chestnuts and oaks still stand on the plateau above the former terraces. Brown's patron was the 7th Duke of Somerset's heir, the 2nd Earl of Egremont – like the 6th Duke, a considerable patron, collector and statesman – who lost little time after inheriting Petworth in 1750 in commissioning Brown to survey the park. Brown's first visit was in October 1751, when he was in his tenth year of working at Stowe, Buckinghamshire, for Viscount Cobham, with whom Egremont had close family connections. Egremont was a keen landscaper and horticulturalist, and his inheritance allowed him to indulge his passion on the grandest scale and in the most fashionable style. Brown's five contracts, worth £5,500 (beginning in 1753 and ending in 1765 two years after the 2nd Earl's death), resulted in one of his supreme creations, which was to be further developed and enriched by the 3rd Earl and his successors in the 19th and 20th centuries. Today, Brown's plan remains the backbone of the Trust's management of the park, but so much had been replanted by the 3rd Earl and others after him that the post-1987 storm survey concluded that none of Brown's trees had survived to be blown down by the winds.

Brown drew up his proposals for the park and Pleasure Ground on a huge map dated 1752. The duke's 'Iron Court' and avenue to the west were replaced by a great expanse of grass, and the formal terraces on the hillside were landscaped into rolling slopes leading the eye towards the new serpentine lake in the middle distance. Ha-

Aerial view of the park to the west and north of the house, showing the lake and the wooded Pleasure Ground

[left]
The Doric Temple, *c.*1740, which was moved by Lancelot Brown from the Upper Terrace to the Pleasure Ground around 1760

has to either side of the house protected the private and kitchen gardens to the south, and the Pleasure Ground to the north, from the deer, which were now able to graze right up to the west front. The margins of the park along the roadside were planted up to give the illusion that the park stretched uninterrupted for miles. The Petworth–Tillington road was moved further away from the house in 1762–4, and the 14-mile-long park wall, already under construction by 1757, was still incomplete in 1779–80. The wider park landscape was clumped, allowing a series of irregular distant views to appear between the trees. To the north-west of the house, the 'Birchen walks', cut into straight and diagonal rides, were preserved within serpentine walks which led around the perimeter, passing the eye-catchers of the Doric summer-house and Brettingham's rotunda. Closer to the house were 'plantations of shrubbs and plants of low growth that will not prevent the prospects' and 'borders adorned with flowering shrubs', many of which were bought from the Kensington nurseryman John Williamson, including *Arbutus*, broom, honeysuckle, Persian jasmine, syringas and roses. Williamson also supplied trees for the Pleasure Ground: Scotch firs, spruce, laurels, planes, larch, limes, cedars and American maples.

About ten years after the 2nd Earl's death in 1763, his cousin, Elizabeth, Duchess of Northumberland, wrote of Brown's 'fine lawn' before the house and of the park as 'very extensive and very beautiful', containing the finest trees 'I ever saw in my life'. This implies that Brown's plantings were already looking established. They were considerably supplemented by the 3rd Earl, who inherited his father's artistic and horticultural proclivities but whose prowess as an agricultural improver was unmatched by any of his line. One aspect of the continual improvements of the park and estate that tends to be overlooked was the provision of employment to the local population.

The 2nd Earl's lake is said to have cost £30,000 and required regular attention to stem the loss of water. The labour costs were such that it was said in Petworth that 'it might have been covered with copper at as little expense'. The 3rd Earl's long reign at Petworth encompassed periods of extreme hardship in the locality arising from poor harvests: in the 1790s, for example, when the price of corn was beyond the means of the poor, Egremont planted potatoes and rice to provide an alternative to bread. His enthusiasms embraced all aspects of ornamental and practical gardening and agriculture. He subscribed to gardening publications (e.g. *The Garden*, *The Botanical Magazine* and *Flora*) and, given his particular interest in arboriculture, owned and was presented with numerous books on the subject.

The 3rd Earl's improvement of the park is indivisible from his management of the agricultural estate. A member of the Board of Agriculture from 1793, he was hailed as 'one of the fathers of modern English agriculture' and was the friend of the famous agriculturalist Arthur Young, whose son, the Rev. Arthur Young, continually cites Egremont's innovations in his *General View of the Agriculture of the County of Sussex*, 1808. The Rev. Arthur Young concluded that 'his Lordship's estates are conducted upon a great scale, in the highest style of improvement'. In 1795 the *Sporting Magazine* stated that 'everything is now conceded at Petworth to grazing and ploughing': for example, in the early 1790s the 3rd Earl began to reclaim the wooded Stag Park. Previously 'an entire forest scene', about 750 acres was 'enclosed and divided into proper fields' once the timber had been sold, 'the underwood grubbed, and burned with charcoal on the spot' and the land had been drained. Like his Wyndham and Percy predecessors, the 3rd Earl never lost an opportunity of acquiring land adjacent to his own, and the Petworth estate now increased rapidly in size, having been built up more slowly during the 18th century and beforehand.

The 3rd Earl was in the vanguard of agricultural improvements that were sweeping the country with the encouragement of theorists (like the Youngs), of the Board of Agriculture and, most effectively, of great landowners (like Egremont himself and his friend, the 5th Duke of Bedford). The park now not only contained deer, but also improved strains of cattle, sheep and even pigs. Young records that 'Lord Egremont has tried a great variety of hogs, and made many experiments'. One of these was to graze the pigs in the park during the summer: 'no corn is given: nothing but grass' after which they were slaughtered. Turner's *Petworth Park* (no.132; Carved Room) includes a group of these grazing pigs in the foreground, which, until recently, were assumed to be sheep. The pigs were housed in a noble piggery, an engraving of which was published by Young. This was surprisingly close to the house, and Egremont's daughter-in-law was once amazed to see 'a sow and her litter of pigs get in through a window and gallop down through the rooms'. Egremont commissioned numerous portraits of his prize cattle (painted by Boultbee and sculpted by Garrard) and his innovations included the breeding of Tibetan shawl goats, depicted in Phillips's 1798 view of the park (no.43; Lord Egremont Collection), whose fleece was prized by London hatters. No avenue of improvement was neglected: trials were carried out (and the results published by Young) on the stocking of fish-ponds, crop rotation, the 'culture and growth' of potatoes, the medicinal use of rhubarb and opium ('the largest quantity of this invaluable drug that was ever cured in this country, was raised in 1797 from the Earl of Egremont's garden at Petworth'); the irrigation and mulching with coal ash of parkland grass; and the use of teams of oxen, instead of horses, to draw wagons, which, despite its inefficiency, was a great enthusiasm of the 3rd Earl's. New machinery was developed such as the Suffolk plough, the Mole-Plough and 'Mr Ducket's Skim-Coulter'

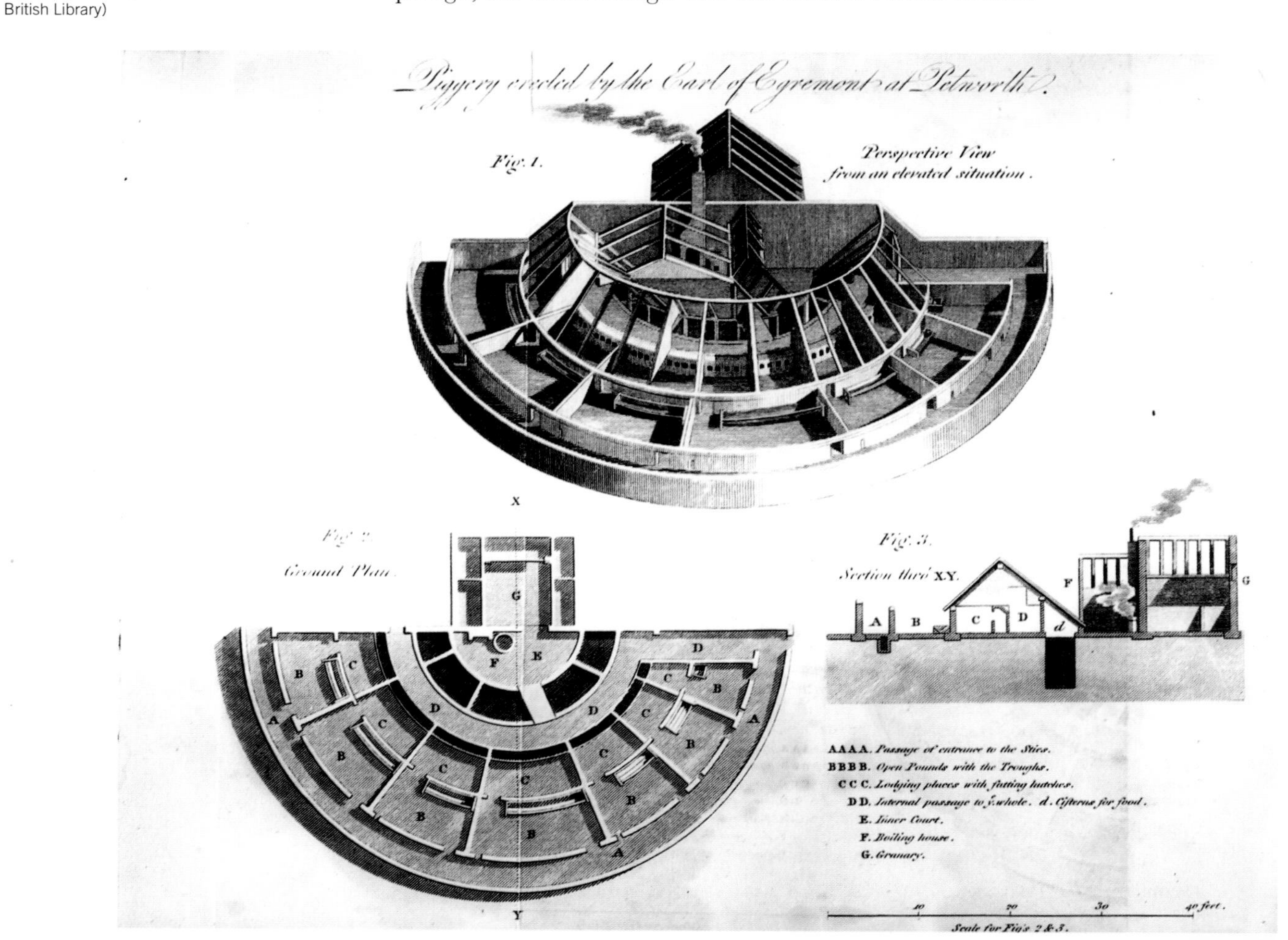

***Piggery erected by the Earl of Egremont at Petworth*, by Neele Strand after C. Blunt, engraved for *A General View of the Agriculture in the County of Sussex*, *c*.1808.** (The British Library)

The gardeners at Petworth in the 1880s with the tools of their trade

('introduced by his Lordship, and with such success, that it was adopted by a number of farmers').

Lord Egremont also supplied Young with statistics, informing him that a farm labourer earned £27 2s per annum, or 10s 5d per week, and that the cost of clothing a family of five children was £8 2s 5d per annum. His concern for the poor was lauded: he supplied them with a 'bounty of clothes' as well as distributing 'three and four times a week, good soup … made of barrelled beef, Scotch barley, and potatoes, besides regaling between three and four hundred families at Christmas with beef and pork pies'. Egremont not only provided labour through the estate but was also an employer on the grandest scale by taking a lead in the local development of roads, and especially canals, which were dug by labourers drawn from among his own workmen. The intention was to connect London with Sussex, which was achieved largely through Egremont's investment in and chairmanship of the Wey, Rother and Arun navigations. As Young observed, this was a considerable boost to the local economy of Surrey and Sussex, doubling the value of many estates, which were able to transport 'timber, and all the production of the soil' to the London market more easily.

Even the radical William Cobbett, who saw the park ('the very finest in the world' within a wall 'nine miles round'), acknowledged Egremont's worthiness 'of this princely estate',[280] which the garden encyclopaedist James Loudon described in 1822 as 'first rate' and a 'truly noble demesne'. The French-American Louis Simond was most impressed by Egremont's planting-up of the Pleasure Ground 'with the largest trees, close together, something like a heavy-timbered American forest… Many of the trees were indeed American. We found here our old acquaintances the hemlock, the black spruce, the tulip-tree, the occidental plane, the acacia, and several kinds of oak. All these trees seem to accommodate themselves extremely well with the climate of England'.[281] Egremont had been active in planting both the park and Pleasure Ground from at least 1773, and in 1804 alone he purchased no fewer than 12,000 ash, fir, larch, birch and hornbeam. He was most interested in the acclimatisation of foreign trees and plants, about which he corresponded with Sir Joseph Banks, and Simond noted that adjacent to the North Gallery was 'the finest conservatory imaginable; the plants in the open ground and not crowded. … I never saw plants in such health and vigour; a heliotrope ten feet high, full of leaves and flowers from the earth to the top, and perfuming the air. … No rare plants, – all for beauty and smell. … The kitchen-garden, all divided into *espalier* walls, covers thirteen acres, – not an inch of which seems unoccupied'.

The kitchen garden was indeed run on princely lines (2,550 asparagus plants were ordered in 1803), incorporating every imaginable variety of vegetables and fruit, while a hot-house in three divisions erected for £400 in 1773 allowed for the growth of exotica such as pineapples. The fame of the kitchen garden reached its apogee in the later 19th century. In 1863, according to the *Journal of Horticulture and the Cottage Gardener*, there was a staff of 20, who produced 260 melons per annum, pineapples, peaches, grapes (plants were found to extend their season) and a huge variety of other fruits and vegetables. Although it was noted that there was a lack of flower borders at Petworth, annuals were grown to provide seed for distribution to estate workers. The 1st Lord Leconfield declared that 'a love of flowers is ever desirable from the very lowest to the very highest'. According to his daughter-in-law, Constance Leconfield, in 1867, the kitchen garden's 'old fashioned border' was preserved by Lady Leconfield, who wished 'not to introduce a ribbon border as was then the great fashion'.[282] In 1878, the *Gardener's Chronicle* also focused on the kitchen garden, which now had a staff of 30, and a green-house was filled with pot plants for display in the house. At about this time, the 2nd Lord Leconfield, having been told that bananas tasted better straight from the tree, sent his gardener to Kew to learn how to grow one. All the necessary paraphernalia was installed at Petworth, including a 'special green house … which might have been the envy of Sir Joseph Paxton himself'. What followed is recounted by his grandson:

> The banana tree was splendid. My grandfather took a lively interest in its progress until, lo and behold, it fructified. 'I will have that banana for dinner tonight', he said as soon as the banana was ripe. And so he did – amid a deathly hush. All were agog. The head gardener himself, controlling a great department of the estate, was not too proud to be there, concealed behind a screen between the dining-room and the serving-room. Even the groom of the chambers broke the habit of a lifetime and turned up sober to watch the event.
>
> The banana was brought in on a lordly dish. My grandfather peeled it with a golden knife, put it in his mouth and carefully tasted it. Whereupon he flung dish, plate, knife, fork and banana on to the floor and shouted, 'Oh God, it tastes just like any other damn banana!' Banana tree and all were ordered to be destroyed. My famous old gardener, Mr Fred Streeter, told me that the banana cost my grandfather some £3,000.[283]

Between the kitchen garden and the south front of the house (an area altered by Salvin in the early 1870s) there was a gigantic dragon of flowers 350 feet wide, coiled upon the grass, who shed 'his skin several times during the year' and who was 'gorgeous with various kinds of bedding plants'.

After 1837 the 3rd Earl's son and grandson, the 1st and 2nd Lords Leconfield, continued to supplement the plantings in the park along traditional lines, eschewing ornamental novelties. Although there are trees surviving from the early 18th century, most of the trees devastated by the storms of the late 1980s had been planted since the turn of the 19th century by the 3rd Lord Leconfield, who succeeded in 1901. Petworth House still stands at the centre of a 12,000-acre agricultural estate, owned by Lord Egremont, whose estate yard undertakes repairs to the house and to estate buildings. Petworth is rare among country houses, whether publicly or privately owned, in retaining its traditional status within the local community, and the long family tradition of allowing full access to the park is upheld by the National Trust.

In 1977 the Petworth landscape was threatened by a proposal to run a bypass through the park between the west front and the lake. This 'route of ignominy' – at its closest only 33 yards from the house – was successfully prevented, but only after a public outcry. The National Trust argued that its custodianship for the nation would have been flouted by the creation of a cut-and-cover tunnel across the very landscape created by 'Capability' Brown and painted by Turner. The Trust threatened to take the matter to Parliament, given that its role as a national guardian of inalienable property rests on an Act of 1907, which can only be revoked by Parliament. In the end, West Sussex County Council was forced to back down. Petworth still does not have a bypass, but the traffic problems in the town have been mitigated by a one-way system, the banning of heavy vehicles and alternative route signing. The Petworth landscape remains inviolate and the park continues to be open to all. As St John Gore eloquently put it, when the park was under threat from the road scheme: 'The art of landscape gardening is a contribution of Britain to the civilization of Europe. And nowhere in the world is there a more serene and precious example of this art than at Petworth, where man's adjustment, as it were, of Nature has conferred on it so breathtaking a beauty.'[284]

Poster, _c._1976, by David Gentleman (b.1930); One of a series of posters in support of the National Trust's campaign to prevent a bypass being driven through 'Capability' Brown's park

[right]
Ionic rotunda in the Pleasure Ground, _c._1760

Notes

1 P.Leslie, ed., *The Letters of John Constable R.A. to C.R.Leslie, R.A., 1826–1837*, London, 1931, p.1834.

2 Petworth House Archives (henceforth PHA).

3 W.H.Coates, ed., *The Journal of Sir Simon D'Ewes*, New York, 1942, p.250: December 1641.

4 De Fonblanque 1887, p.xxii.

5 *The Dolorous Death and Most Lamentable Chance of the Most Honorable Earl of Northumberland* (1489).

6 Brenan 1902, p.160.

7 *Letters and Papers, Foreign and Domestic of the Reign of Henry VIII*, Public Record Office, London, 1965, vol.IV, pt.2, p.1058.

8 British Library, Egerton MSS 2074, fol.95.

9 G.B.Harrison, ed., *[The 9th Earl of Northumberland's]Advice to his Son*, London, 1930, p.81.

10 Ibid., pp.78–84.

11 British Library, Hargrave MSS 226, fols.241–3.

12 Batho 1960, p.251.

13 John Wallis, quoted in W.Hutchinson, *A View of Northumberland*, Newcastle, 1776, vol.II (1778), p.240 (note).

14 Batho 1962, p.119.

15 Ibid., p.114.

16 Edward, Earl of Clarendon, *The History of the Rebellion and Civil Wars in England*, Oxford, 1707, vol.III, p.270.

17 Quoted in De Fonblanque 1887, p.474.

18 Edward, Earl of Clarendon, *The History of the Rebellion and Civil Wars in England*, Oxford, 1843, vol.VI, p. 372.

19 *The Works of Sir William Temple, Bart.*, London, 1750, vol. II, p.220 (Temple to the 11th Earl of Northumberland, The Hague, 17 June 1670).

20 R.S.Magurn, ed., *The Letters of Peter Paul Rubens*, Cambridge, Mass., 1955, p.322 (Letter to Peiresc, 9 August 1629).

21 Wood 1994, pp.283–4, fig.3, p.303 (no.4), p.304 (no.4), p.316 note 17, with references to previous literature. The picture was discovered when at Albury Park, and its history and importance recognised, by M.Jaffé, 'The Picture of the Secretary of Titian', *The Burlington Magazine*, vol.CVIII, March 1966, pp.114–27.

22 K. Andrews, *Adam Elsheimer: Paintings – Drawings – Prints*, 1977, cat. nos.17 A–H; Wood 1994, pp.282–5, p.305 (no.40), p.316 (no.16); Laing 1995 (nos.59 a–h).

23 Wood 1994, p.284, p.303 (no.3); p.304 (no.5); p.316 note 21, with references to previous literature. For the *Corsini Madonna*, see A.Natali and A.Cecchi, *Andrea del Sarto: Catalogo completo dei dipinti*, Florence, 1989, no.18, in which it was wrongly located at the Courtauld Institute, where it had been restored. Regrettably, the Petworth picture, which shows fine underdrawing and a significant *pentimento*, was not requested for loan when the Louvre and Munich versions of the *Madonna and Child, St Elizabeth and John the Baptist, and Angels* were juxtaposed in the exhibition *Divinely Painted—Andrea del Sarto: The Holy Family in Munich and Paris*, Alte Pinakothek, Munich, 2009. The Petworth picture was reproduced in the catalogue: C.Syre, J.Schmidt and H.Stege, eds., *Göttlich gemalt: Andrea del Sarto: Die Heilige Familie in Paris und München*, exh. cat., Munich, 2009, fig.28, p.49; see also p.50 and p.51, notes 66 and 67. I am grateful to Dr. Patrick Dietemann for giving me a copy of this exhibition catalogue.

24 For the 1671 inventory of the Northumberland Collection at Northumberland House, Petworth and Syon, see Alnwick Castle Archives (ACA) 72, MS 107, GC26, published in full in Wood 1994, pp.304–8, appendix III.

25 ACA, MS Syon House U.1.5, unnumbered; published in Wood 1994, p.109, appendix IV, no.8.

26 Rowell 2003.

27 Wood 1994, pp.285–6, figs.5–9 and p.317, notes 32–8.

28 Formerly Petworth no.322; Collins Baker 1920, p.130; Wood 1994, p.304, (no.3), p.322, note 173.

29 In [A.E. Knox] *Catalogue of Pictures in Petworth House, Sussex*, 1856, p.33, as by Titian. Collins Baker, however, inexplicably demoted it (despite Waagen's support of the ascription) to 'North Italian School, XVIth Century', whilst saying: 'Caprioli also has been suggested' (Collins Baker 1920, p.62). Rehabilitated by Anthony Blunt and by St John Gore (Gore 1977, p.352 and fig.17), it was exhibited, as one of seven early portraits by Titian, at the Palais Fesch-Musée des Beaux-Arts, Ajaccio, 26 June–27 September 2010: see exh. cat., *Titien: l'étrange homme au gant*, Milan, 2010, pp.44, 130 and fig.35. See also Wood 1994, p.306, no.72, and p.322, note 212.

30 Alnwick 72, MS 107, GC 26, Appendix III in Wood 1994.

31 PHA 5869, transcribed in full in Appendix IV, no.47 in Wood 1994.

32 PHA 5931, Appendix IV, no.60 in Wood 1994.

33 PHA 5788, Appendix IV, no.66 in Wood 1994.

34 PHA 5893, Appendix IV, no.51 in Wood 1994.

35 See Rowell 2003 for the dating of these picture frames.

36 E.S. de Beer, ed., *The Diary of John Evelyn*, Oxford, 1959, p.391 (entry for 7 June 1658).

37 W.Bray, ed., *Memoirs of John Evelyn*, London, 1827, vol.IV, p.69.

38 *Calendar of the MSS of the Marquess of Ormonde*, RCHM, 1908, vol.V, p.475.

39 P.Rogers, ed., *Jonathan Swift: The Complete Poems*, Harmondsworth, 1983, p.119.

40 G.L.Craik, *Romance of the Peerage*, London, 1849, vol.IV, p.351.

41 'Remarks on the Characters of the Court of Queen Anne', *The Works of Jonathan Swift, D.D.*, New York, 1861, vol.II, p.572.

42 Lord Hardwicke; in a note in Gilbert Burnet's *History of His Own Time*, Oxford, 1823, vol.VI, p.13.

43 C.H.Firth, ed., Lord Macaulay, *The History of England*, London, 1914, vol.II, p.918.

44 PHA 246 (30 September 1693): 'twenty Pounds which was paid to Mr. Maro'.

45 PHA 6263.

46 W.S Lewis, ed., *The Yale Edition of Horace Walpole's Correspondence*, 48 vols, New Haven 1937–83, vol.IX, p.97 (letter to George Montagu dated 26 August 1749).

47 PHA 652 (1685–6).

48 PHA 171.

49 PHA 5377, Leconfield MSS, *Catalogus Librorum Bibliothecae Petworthianae* (*c.*1690?).

50 Rowell 2003; Collins Baker 1920, pp.20–21; W. Nisser, *Michael Dahl and the contemporary Swedish School of Painting*, Uppsala, 1927, pp.91–7, pls.XIII–XVIII.

51 Wood 1994, p.307 (no.98).

52 *Walpole Society: Vertue Note Books*, vol.V, 1938 (reprinted 1968), pp.54–56.

53 We do know, again from Vertue, however, that early on the 6th Duke of Somerset acted on Closterman's advice when buying pictures, including a reputed Guercino of *Lot and his Daughters* in one of the later annual sales held by the engraver-dealer Edward [Le] Davis (active 1671–after 1691). He agreed on the equally remarkable price of 200 guineas for this, but, between making the agreement and collecting the picture, the value of the guinea had been altered to 26 shillings, instead of 21. The duke refused to pay for the painting at this new rate, but Closterman did pay (retaining it till his death), which so enraged the duke that he cut off all communication with Closterman, and not only sat to Dahl thereafter, ordering several replicas of the portrait to give away, but also commissioned the whole-length 'Beauties' from him. The duke may even have been discouraged by this from making further acquisitions of pictures for a period, but at the actor Thomas Betterton's posthumous sale in 1710, he had recovered his confidence sufficiently to pay £44 for William Dobson's unusual *Self-Portrait with Sir Charles Cotterell and Nicholas Lanier (?)*. He evidently had a taste for Dobson, since he also seems to have acquired the portrait called *A Father sitting in his chair with his son standing behind him* attributed to Dobson then and since (both still in the collection of the Duke of Northumberland).

54 See Jackson-Stops 1980a, p.799.

55 British Library, Add. MSS 15776.

56 W.S. Lewis, ed., *The Yale Edition of Horace Walpole's Correspondence*, vol.XL, New Haven, 1980, pp.318–19 (John Bromfield to Horace Walpole, 14 April 1764). Walpole further recounts obtaining a partial list, and himself making a catalogue.

57 PHA 244.

58 The duke also bought at least one piece of antique sculpture: 'a Faustines head, Antient', which was acquired in 1683, and '8 Roman heads' were bought in 1694–5. Grinling Gibbons supplied 'statues' in 1692 and in 1700 £100 was laid out 'to pay a Dutchman for Casting of Statues'. In 1724 the duke paid £43 for 'a large marble statue' (probably antique) and £6 for a 'marble head representing the Late King William'. The latter is probably not the Bernini-esque head by the Huguenot sculptor Honoré Pelle (Grand Stairs), as this is now considered to depict James II.

59 PHA 246 (18 Feb 1693): 'necessary Charges when the King was at Petworth'; and PHA 173 (1694–5): 'to the Cooke who assisted to dress the King's dinner 10s'.

60 British Library, Add. MSS 15776.

61 For Holkham, Lord Leicester, and Brettingham, see L.Schmidt, C.Keller and P.Feversham, eds., *Holkham*, Munich, Berlin, London and New York, 2005.

62 Admiral the Hon. Edward Boscawen to his wife, 11 October 1757, quoted in C.W.James, *Chief Justice Coke His Family and Descendants at Holkham*, London, 1929, p.273. The journey to Norfolk is noted in the 2nd Earl's accounts: PHA 7462 'Journey to Norfolk & back £40.12.0' (18 October 1757).

63 PHA 7450 (15 March 1735).

64 PHA 7451 (17 March 1741).

65 W.S. Lewis, ed., op.cit., vol.XX, p.11, (letter to Sir Horace Mann, 15 December 1748).

66 PHA 7456 (21 February 1751) and (18 January 1751) respectively.

67 PHA 7454.

68 PHA 6266.

69 For Egremont House and its collection, see Rowell 1998.

70 PHA 5742; 2nd Earl of Egremont's notebook listing his purchase of pictures, the place, date and cost (1748/9–63).

71 W.S. Lewis, ed., op.cit., vol.XXI, p.172 (letter to Sir Horace Mann, 9 February 1758).

72 See Rowell 1998.

73 See Laing 1995, no.36, pp.102–3.

74 PHA 5742.

75 PHA 6267 (dated 5 December 1764).

76 PHA 6266.

77 She did a charming head-and-shoulders – unusually, in oils – of her eldest son as a baby (no.694*; White Library; Lord Egremont Collection).

78 The portrait of the countess was exhibited in *William Hoare of Bath, R.A., 1707–1792*, Victoria Art Gallery, Bath (catalogue by E.Newby), 1990, no.20.

79 From a sale of pictures formerly in the collection of the earls of Leicester at Penshurst.

80 Norman's voluminous bill is PHA 6264, no.184.

81 John Nicols, *Illustrations of the Literary History of the Eighteenth Century*, London, 1818, vol.III, p.728.

82 For these statues restored by Cavaceppi and the 2nd Earl's collection of statuary, see Proudfoot and Rowell 1997.

83 J.Kenworthy-Browne, 'Matthew Brettingham's Rome Account Book, 1747–1754', *Walpole Society*, vol.XLIX, 1983, p.62.

84 Quoted in *The Universal British Directory*, London, n.d., vol.IV, p.216.

85 Annabel Yorke, Lady Polwarth to her mother, Marchioness Grey (20 August 1776); Bedfordshire Record Office (Lucas MSS L/30/9/60/83).

86 *The Universal British Directory*, London, n.d., vol.IV, p.216.

87 Left outdoors and unprotected at Lowther Castle, it has become a piece of mere garden sculpture, and is now in the grounds of Helbeck Hall, Westmorland.

88 G.Waagen, *Treasures of Art in Great Britain*, London, 1854, vol.III, p.32.

89 W.S. Lewis, ed., op.cit., vol.XXII, p.158–9 (letter to Sir Horace Mann, 1 September 1763).

90 M.A.Lower, *The Worthies of Sussex*, Lewes, 1865, p.90.

91 Ibid.

92 W.Bissell Pope, ed., *The Diary of Benjamin Robert Haydon*, vol.III, 1825–1832, Cambridge Mass., 1963, p.167 (15 November 1826).

93 Ibid. (18 November 1826).

94 *The Greville Memoirs*, London, 1885, part 2, vol.I, p.25 (14 November 1837).

95 L. Simond, *Journal of a Tour and Residence in Great Britain*, Edinburgh, 1817, 2nd edn., vol.II, p.325.

96 T.Taylor, ed., *Autobiographical Recollections by the late Charles Robert Leslie, R.A.*, London, 1860, vol.I, pp.102–3.

97 For the 3rd Earl in general, see especially Egremont 1985, Laing 2001a and Rowell 2004.

98 L.Lagrange, *Les Vernet: Joseph Vernet et la peinture au XVIIIe siècle*, Paris, 1864. pp.171, 351, no.262.

99 J.Egerton, *George Stubbs, Painter. Catalogue Raisonné*, New Haven and London, 2007, no.154, pp.350–51, suggests that *Trentham* was painted for one of its two owners in the first half of 1773, Thomas Foley, later 2nd Baron Foley, since it was only in 1777 that the horse changed hands, and only by 1788 that he was in the 3rd Earl's stud at Petworth. Since the *Pomeranian Dog* (which is for some reason omitted from Judy Egerton's catalogue) is dated the same year, might both the pictures have been acquired by Lord Egremont from the indebted Foley?

100 The sale, containing 60 pictures and just one piece of sculpture, was at Christie's, 8–11 August 1785 (Lugt 3931).

101 7–8 March, 1794 (Lugt 5166). The only copy of the catalogue, with several buyer's names and prices, is in Christie's London archive.

102 I am grateful to Patricia Ferguson for her report on these services, for which see PHA 8566 (Bills for tours of France 1774/5) and D.Peters, *Sèvres Plates and Services of the 18th century*, Little Berkhamsted, 2005, vol.I, 74–4, p.509 and vol.II, 74–5, p.511.

103 Cited in Wyndham 1950, vol.II, p.217.

104 W.S. Lewis, ed., op.cit., vol.XXV, p.68 (letter to Sir Horace Mann, 6 July 1780).

105 Ibid., vol.XXV, p.75 (letter to Sir Horace Mann, 24 July 1780).

106 K.Garlick and A.Macintyre, eds., *The Diary of Joseph Farington*, New Haven and London, 1979, vol.III, pp.1113–4 (18 December 1798).

107 Lord Granville Leveson Gower (1st Earl Granville), *Private Correspondence, 1781 to 1821*, London, 1916, vol.II, p.474.

108 Creevey MSS (18 August 1828); Private Collection.

109 The Earl of Ilchester, ed., *Elizabeth Lady Holland to her Son, 1821–1845*, London, 1946, pp.72, 87.

110 K.Garlick and A.Macintyre, eds., *The Diary of Joseph Farington*, New Haven and London, 1979, vol.III, p.1115 (20 December 1798).

111 W.B.Pope, ed., *The Diary of Benjamin Robert Haydon*, Cambridge, Mass., 1983, vol.III (*1825–1832*), p.166.

112 T.Taylor, ed., *Life of Benjamin Robert Haydon*, London, 1853, vol.III, p.71 (1837).

113 Earl of Ilchester, ed., *The Journal of the Hon. Henry Edward Fox*, 1923, pp.183–5.

114 H.Reeve, ed., *The Greville Memoirs: A Journal of the Reigns of King George IV and King William IV*, London, 1874, vol.II, p.337.

115 W.S. Lewis, ed., op.cit., vol.XXXII, p.154 (letter to the Countess of Upper Ossory, 7 October 1773).

116 Creevey MSS (18 August 1828); Private Collection.

117 J.Gore, ed., *Creevey's Life and Times*, London, 1934, p.275.

118 Creevey MSS (18 August 1828); Private Collection.

119 J.Gore, ed., *Creevey's Life and Times*, London, 1934, p.277.

120 Ibid., p.276.

121 H.Reeve, ed., *The Greville Memoirs: A Journal of the Reigns of King George IV and King William IV*, London, 1874, vol.II, p.336 (20 December 1832).

122 William Hayley, *The Life of George Romney*, Chichester, 1809, p.234.

123 Ibid., p.263.

124 C.R.Leslie, *Memoirs of the Life of John Constable*, London, 1845, p.255.

125 T.Taylor, ed., *Autobiographical Recollections by the late Charles Robert Leslie, R.A.*, London, 1860, vol.II, p.220.

126 The literature on Turner has increased immeasurably in the last 40 years. See especially Youngblood 1983 and Laing 2001 a and b. See also M. Butlin and E. Joll, *The Paintings of J.M.W. Turner*, New Haven and London, 1977; Butlin, Luther and Warrell 1989; and Rowell, Warrell and Blayney Brown 2002.

127 For the location of Turner's Studio, see Rowell, Warrell and Blayney Brown 2002, p.150.

128 J.Gore, ed., *Creevey's Life and Times*, London, 1934, p.274; 1948, p.291; T.Taylor, ed., *Autobiographical Recollections by the late Charles Robert Leslie, R.A.*, London, 1860, p.103.

129 W.B.Pope, ed., *The Diary of Benjamin Robert Haydon*, Cambridge, Mass., 1983, vol.III (*1825–1832*), pp.166–71.

130 V.Surtees, ed., *The Diaries of George Price Boyce*, Norwich, 1980, p.17 (30 June 1857).

131 It was Francis Russell who first observed, at a National Trust's Arts Panel visit to Petworth in 2002, when the Turners had just been fixed once again in their original positions in the panelling, that the reason for the uncommonly low placing of Turner's four pictures in the Carved Room was so that they could be seen at eye level by those sitting at the dinner table, who could turn from the two views of the park to the actual landscape, with the vanishing point at the same height.

132 C.R.Leslie, ed., *Memoirs of the Life of John Constable Esq., R.A.*, London, 1845, p.258.

133 Ibid., pp.257–8.

134 R.B.Beckett, ed., *John Constable's Correspondence*, Ipswich, 1962–8, vol.II, p.367.

135 T.Taylor, ed., *Autobiographical Recollections by the late Charles Robert Leslie, R.A.*, London, 1860, vol.I, p.105.

136 'Recollections of Leslie', *Quarterly Review*, vol.II, 1860, p.448.

137 Rowell 1993.

138 T.Taylor, ed., *Life of Benjamin Robert Haydon*, London, 1853, vol.III, p. 368.

139 G.Jones, *Sir Francis Chantrey, R.A.*, London, 1849, p.198.

140 T.Taylor, ed., *Life of Benjamin Robert Haydon*, London, 1853, vol.II, p.137.

141 J.Holland, *Memorials of Sir Francis Chantrey*, London, 1851, p.215.

142 W.B.Pope, ed., *The Diary of Benjamin Robert Haydon*, Cambridge, Mass., 1963, vol.III, p.172.

143 *Report of the Proceedings in the Court for the Relief of Insolvent Debtors in the matter of John Edward Carew, An Insolvent Debtor*, London, 1842, pp.240 and 242.

144 Ibid., pp.233–4.

145 See Rowell 1993, p.33.

146 *Report of the Proceedings in the Court for the Relief of Insolvent Debtors in the matter of John Edward Carew, An Insolvent Debtor*, London, 1842.

147 M.Busco, *Sir Richard Westmacott, Sculptor*, 1994, pp.27, 93, 103–4, 110–12, and figs.93, 99.

148 The Earl of Ilchester, ed., *Elizabeth Lady Holland to her Son*, London, 1946, p.72.

149 T.Taylor, ed., *Autobiographical Recollections by the late Charles Robert Leslie, R.A.*, London, 1860, vol.I, p.102.

150 C.Greville, *The Greville Memoirs: A Journal of the Reign of Queen Victoria*, London, 1885, vol.I, p.24.

151 T. Taylor, ed., *Autobiographical Recollections by the late Charles Robert Leslie, R.A.*, London, 1860, vol.I, p.163.

152 *Nimrod's Hunting Tours*, London, 1835, p.106.

153 Egremont 1968, p.45.

154 G. Waagen, *Treasures of Art in Great Britain*, London, 1854, vol.III, p.32.

155 Leconfield 1938, p.50.

156 Ibid., p.50–51.

157 Ibid., p.42.

158 Egremont 1968, p.55.

159 Dakers 1993.

160 Egremont 1968, p.67.

161 Ibid., p.61.

162 Ibid., p.56.

163 T.L. Ribblesdale, *Impressions and Memories*, London, 1927, p.176.

164 Egremont 1968, p.57.

165 Ibid., p.61.

166 Ibid., p.62–3.

167 Ibid., p.198.

168 J. Lees-Milne, *Caves of Ice*, London, 1984, p.132.

169 Egremont 1968, p.200.

170 Ibid., p.204.

171 For this and the following references, see Blunt 1980.

172 Garnett 2004.

173 Rowell, Warrell and Blayney Brown 2002.

174 There is no recent catalogue of the pictures at Petworth, and Collins-Baker's catalogue (Collins-Baker 1920) has therefore not been superseded. For lists of pictures in the public rooms with summary descriptions, see Jackson-Stops 1993 and Rowell 1997. As for antique sculpture, the first comprehensive account was Wyndham 1915, and the most recent is Raeder, Erhardt and Eder 2000. Summary lists of antique and Neo-classical sculpture may again be found in Jackson-Stops 1993 and Rowell 1997. For general histories of the collection, see Gore 1977, Rowell 1997 and Laing 1995, pp.233–4.

175 Klinge 1991, no.76, pp.220–3; Vegelin van Claerbergen 2006, no.2, pp.70–3.

176 David Teniers, *THEATRUM PICTORIUM In quo exhibentur ipsius manu deliniatae, eiusque curâ in aes incisae Picturae Archetipae Italicae, quas ipse Ser[mus] Archidux in Pinacothecam suam Bruxellis collegit*, Antwerp, 1660. There were also editions in Dutch, French and Spanish. For a full description of this book and the associated paintings, see Klinge 1991, pp.278–97; and Vegelin van Claerbergen 2006, no.5, pp.80–1 and *passim*.

177 P. McEvansoneya, 'The Sequestration and Dispersal of the Buckingham Collection', *Journal of the History of Collections*, vol.VIII, no.2, 1996, pp.133–54.

178 Teniers's engraved depiction of the Stallburg in Vienna is reproduced in Vegelin van Claerbergen 2006, fig.13, p.25; and Alden R. Gordon, 'Depictions of Display: Toward a Census of Engraved Images of Interiors', in S. Bracken, A. Gáldy, A. Turpin, eds., *Collecting and the Princely Apartment*, Newcastle-upon-Tyne, 2011, pp.108–9 and fig.22.

179 O. Millar, *Zoffany and his Tribuna*, London, 1967.

180 An autograph variant of the Petworth picture (Kunsthistorisches Museum, Vienna) is of the same size and of nearly identical composition with the visiting bishop replaced by a classical bust on a partly gilded Italianate carved plinth of a type depicted in other views of the gallery.

181 C. Rowell, 'A seventeenth-century "Cabinet" restored: The Green Closet at Ham House', *Apollo*, vol.CXLIII, April 1996, pp.18–24.

182 F. Scholten, ed., *Adriaen de Vries, 1556–1626*, exh. cat. (Amsterdam, Stockholm and Los Angeles), Zwolle, 1998, no.16, pp.154–5 (entry by Frits Scholten and Thomas Dacosta Kaufmann).

183 For example the table is depicted very clearly in the picture in the Bayerische Staatsgemäldesammlung, Munich; see Klinge 1991, no.79, pp.228–9.

184 Proudfoot and Rowell 1997, p.184 and plates 77–78.

185 Rowell 1998.

186 Henry Wyndham Phillips's plan and list is V&A MS 86 FF67; see also Rowell 1993. The 1856 catalogue is PHA 7519.

187 Jackson-Stops 1985, no.226, p.302 (entry by Carlos Picon). See also Alain Pasquier and Jean-Luc Martinez, eds., *Praxitèle*, exh. cat., Louvre, Paris, 2007, no.18, pp.116–7 (entry by A. Pasquier). Pasquier describes the 'Leconfield Aphrodite' as the 'sole of all the Aphrodites which puts us in direct contact with the manner of the master'.

188 For a history of the White and Gold Room and the arrangement of the pictures, see Rowell, Warrell and Blayney Brown 2002, pp.100–05.

189 Quoted in C. Brown and H. Vlieghe, eds., *Van Dyck 1599–1641*, exh. cat., Antwerp and London, 1999, no.98, pp.322–3 (entry by Judy Egerton).

190 For this aspect of the 10th Earl's Van Dyck portraits, see Rowell 2003.

191 Ibid., fig.4, p.42.

192 Rowell, Warrell and Blayney Brown 2002, pp.100–101, figs. 97 and 98.

193 Ibid., cat.38 and fig.84.

194 For a full discussion of the genesis of Turner's Carved Room pictures and for images of all the relevant paintings, see Rowell, Warrell and Blayney Brown 2002.

195 For the series of Carved Room pictures and the preliminary versions, see Rowell, Warrell and Blayney Brown 2002, pp.30–9, figs.22–31; pp.120–31 and *passim*.

196 Ibid., fig.1, p.10 (painting by S.W. Parrott, 1846).

197 John Gore ed., *Creevey's Life and Times*, London, 1934, p.278.

198 Rowell, Warrell and Blayney Brown 2002, cat.44, fig.99.

199 Rowell, Warrell and Blayney Brown 2002, cat.31, fig.124.

200 A pair of Leslie's watercolours of details of the *State Bed* was acquired from the Gallery Lingard by Lord and Lady Egremont in 1996. These were probably lot 209 – 'Studies of the King of Spain's Bed at Petworth' – among 20 or so such studies of items at Petworth in Leslie's posthumous sale, 2nd day, 26 April 1860.

201 T. Taylor, ed., *Autobiographical Recollections by the late Charles Robert Leslie, R.A.*, London, 1860.

202 A. Wheelock, S. Barnes and J. Held, eds., *Anthony van Dyck*, exh. cat., National Gallery of Art, Washington, DC, 1990, nos.28.29, pp.154–5 (entry by Susan Barnes); and Laing 1995, no.2, pp.20–1 (Robert Shirley).

203 Waagen 1854, vol.III, p.40.

204 The studies for the portraits are reproduced in Wheelock, Barnes and Held 1990, p.154.

205 The frame was originally supplied for the good copy of Holbein's *Henry VIII* (no.135, Carved Room).

206 Rowell 1998, fig.7 and caption, p.19.

207 For the Creevey quotations, see Rowell, Warrell and Blayney Brown 2002, pp.22 and 18.

208 Wyndham 1915, nos.81, 82 A, B, pp.133–4 and plates.

209 Accounts (18 June 1582–Lady Day 1583) of William Wycliffe, cofferer to the 8th Earl, Syon House MSS U. 11.

210 Wallis 1951, and H.Wallis, 'Further Light on the Molyneux Globes', *The Geographical Journal*, vol.XII, September 1955, pp.304–11.

211 A.Read, *The Chirurgicall Lectures of Tumors and Ulcers*, London 1635, p.307.

212 And again in 1985 and 2009. Christie's, London, *Fine French and Continental Furniture European Carpets*, 12 December 1985, lot 134; and Christie's, London, *Important European Furniture, Sculpture and Clocks*, 9 July 2009, lot 94 (£289,250).

213 Batho 1960, p.259. The books are at Petworth (Lord Egremont Collection): J.Androuet du Cerceau, *Livre d'Architecture*, Paris 1582, which is bound with J.Vredeman de Vries, *Coenotaphiorum libellus*, 1563, and *Panoplia seu armentarium ac ornamenta*, 1572; De Vries's *Perspective*, Leyden, 1599 and (with P.Vredeman de Vries) *Architectura*, The Hague, 1606.

214 V&A no.57–1881. This is Roman, *c.*1580. Now stripped of its later overall gilding, the resemblance to the Petworth table is more manifest.

215 PHA 6261.

216 For the Lacock set, see E.Debruijn et al., '[National Trust] Acquisitions', *National Trust Historic Houses & Collections Annual 2010, Apollo*, 2010, p.36, fig.4 (entry by C.Rowell). For the V&A chair, see C.Wilk, ed., *Western Furniture 1350 to the Present Day in the Victoria and Albert Museum London*, London, 1996, pp.52–3 (entry by Tessa Murdoch). For the *sgabelli*, see Jackson-Stops 1977b, p.358; and Jackson-Stops 1985, nos.59 and 60, p.135 (entries by G.Jackson-Stops); and M.Drury, 'Italian Furniture in National Trust Houses', *Furniture History*, vol.XX, 1984, p.39.

217 V&A no.7179–1860 and 7183–1860. See M. Ajmar-Wollheim and F.Dennis, eds., *At Home in Renaissance Italy*, exh. cat., Victoria & Albert Museum, London, 2006, cat. no.130, pl.15.23.

218 PHA 156; 1684.

219 PHA 230.

220 PHA 245 (25 November 1692): '£300 to Mr Turnear for New Painting and gilding the Chappell and to a french man for gilt sconces'.

221 For the original Carved Room and for its later extension and alteration, see Rowell 2000 and Rowell 2002.

222 H.Walpole to G.Montagu, 26 August 1749, in W.S. Lewis and R.S. Brown, eds., *Horace Walpole's Correspondence with George Montagu*, Edinburgh and London, 1941, vol.I, pp.97–8; and in W.S. Lewis, op. cit., vol.IX, pp.97–8.

223 H. Walpole, *Anecdotes of Painting in England*, London, 1763, iii, pp.85–6.

224 PHA 245; 29 December 1692: 'Fourscore pounds to pay Mr Glausterman for Drawing my Lord Dukes and his Sisters Picktures being whole lengths £80'. PHA 245; 10 December 1692: 'a bill paid to Mr. Gibbons for Carveing £150'.

225 G.Jackson-Stops 1984, p.1700 and fig.10.

226 PHA 248 (6 January 1695): 'To Mr Gibbons for two fine Jaspar Stone Tables 6f. long x 3f. x ½ over eache £40'.

227 One of the outstanding pieces attributable to Jensen – a marquetry table with a folding top, incorporating the cipher of the Duchess of Somerset beneath a coronet, *c.*1695 (Lord Egremont Collection) – is reproduced in Jackson-Stops 1977b, fig.6, p.359.

228 Jackson-Stops 1984, p.1698.

229 M.Snodin, ed., *Rococo: Art and Design in Hogarth's England*, exh. cat., London, Victoria and Albert Museum, 1984, L49, p.178 (entry by John Hardy); and Jackson-Stops 1984.

230 The drawings are in the Harry Ransom Research Center, The University of Texas at Austin. In a letter to Gervase Jackson-Stops (10 September 1992; NT Archive) Elizabeth Neubauer wrote: 'I have looked into the matter of the Ritson attribution.... There are no signatures and indeed no evidence as to their attribution, though it would appear that these drawings are in fact by Ritson ... there is no existing provenance of the drawings in our records.'

231 Jackson-Stops 1977a, p.330.

232 PHA 5229.

233 PHA 7454 (20 December 1750).

234 Rowell 1998, p.18 and fig.6.

235 The following entry may be relevant: PHA 3117 (4 November, 1721) Wm. Hall: 'Making Frames for Marble Tables, £6.8.8'.

236 Rowell, Warrell and Blayney Brown 2002, p.85 and figs 84–5.

237 For Egremont House, see Rowell 1998, pp.15–21.

238 A. Coleridge, 'Some Mid-Georgian Cabinet-Makers at Holkham', *Apollo*, vol.LXXIX, February 1964, fig. 4.

239 Jackson-Stops 1977, pp.362–3.

240 P. Ward-Jackson, *English Furniture Designs of the 18th Century*, London, 1958, fig. 52.

241 Jackson-Stops 1977, p.364 and fig.16.

242 PHA 3131 (23 June 1753): James Whittle £88.9.0 'in full for Gilt Frames'.

243 See Jackson-Stops 1977, p.365 and fig.21.

244 G.Borghini, ed., *Marmi Antichi*, Rome 1997, no. 14, pp. 155–6 (entry by M.Marchei).

245 For a photograph of one of the tables with its long drawer open, see W.Rieder, 'Gervase Jackson-Stops 1947–1995', *Apollo*, vol.CXLIII, April 1996, p.3.

246 For the 2nd Earl as a collector of French furniture, see Hughes 2008a, pp.58–66.

247 PHA 7451; 17 March 1741.

248 PHA 3131; March 1752.

249 PHA.

250 Hughes 2008a, pp.65–6.

251 PHA 5951: John Kerr ('£258.17.5 for Furniture'). The *Dictionary of English Furniture Makers, London 1660–1840*, Leeds, 1986, states that these Square Dining Room chairs were supplied in 1801, but Kerr's six 1801 chairs had 'Square Stuf'd Backs Coverd with the best Red Morocco Leather £24' and therefore cannot be the ones in the Square Dining Room. For other orders to Kerr, see PHA 5950 (21 March 1801), PHA 5954 ('for London house £489.15', 1802) and PHA 8055 (1787–90).

252 Gilbert 1978, vol.I, pp.282–6, where the 3rd Earl's account with Chippendale is published in full (PHA 6611).

253 See Gilbert 1978, vol.I, pp.164–5 and vol.II, fig.386: '21 July 1764 Mr Chippendale's Bill Stools for the Library [£]38 15 –... Saunders for Carriage of the Stools from London 18 [s]'.

254 PHA 6608.

255 See Hughes 2008b, pp.59–60, figs. 2 and 3; and C.Rowell, 'French Furniture at Uppark: Sir Harry Fetherstonhaugh and his Friends in Post-Revolutionary Paris', *Furniture History*, vol.XLIII, 2007, pp.272, 290, n.32.

256 PHA 5959 (28 October 1807): 'A very handsome Mahogany Cylinder Writing Desk with small drawers inside, large drawers on each side, with Kneehole, on strong castors... £19'.

257 Hughes 2008b, pp.60–2 and fig.4.

258 For the Carved Room and Leslie's oil painting, see Rowell, Warrell and Blayney Brown 2002, pp.120–31 and fig.124.

259 Versailles (RMN 75 DN 2275).

260 For the Louvre table, see the online catalogue entry at louvre.fr.

261 Ibid.

262 For the Petworth table and the related examples described here, see J.-C.Gaffiot, *Le Mobilier d'Apparat des Palais Lorrains sous les Règnes des ducs Léopold et François III (1698–1737)*, Metz, 2009, pp.90–1 and figs (the Petworth table is also illustrated on the front cover). See also Hughes 2008b, pp.58–63.

263 For the reference and a general account of Sené's work, see François, comte de Salverte, *Les Ébénistes du XVIIIe Siècle: leurs Oeuvres et leurs Marques*, Paris and Brussels, 1927, pp.319–20 and pl.LXII.

264 For the pair of commodes made for Louis XIV, see D.Meyer, *Versailles: Furniture of the Royal Palace, 17th and 18th Centuries*, vol.I, Dijon, 2002, no.9.

265 For example, the drawer linings are not of walnut, but of a South American wood resembling kingwood or *palissandre*. There is also a stepped gilt-bronze moulding immediately below the marble top, where the Versailles pair has plain ebony veneer. There are also small differences in the gilt-bronze mounts, which include the lack in the Petworth version of a flower motif in the centre of the square cartouche above the spiral leg supports.

266 J.Guiffrey, *Comptes des Bâtiments du Roi sous le règne de Louis XIV*, Paris, 1881–1901, V, col.241.

267 Paris, Archives Nationales, O1 3336 fol.196; quoted in P. Hughes, 'The Grand Trianon Commodes by André-Charles Boulle and their Influence', *Furniture History*, vol.XLIII, 2007, pp.195–203.

268 For example, see Hughes, ibid., fig.6.

269 For references to several antique Roman examples, see Hughes, ibid., p.196 and p.210 n.6.

270 *Specimens of Cabinet Work and of Studies from the Schools of Art*, exh. cat., Gore House, Kensington, London, 1853, p.20.

271 See D.Dubon and T.Dell, *The Frick Collection, An Illustrated Catalogue, vol. V, Furniture: Italian and French*, New York, 1992, pp.233–46 (entry by Theodore Dell). Dell doubts that the model for the two copies was the Petworth commode, on the basis of minor variations in the mounts of the Frick copies, but he does allow the possibility that it was indeed the model. There is a provenance note, dated 1954, from the vendor (the New York and London dealer, Duveen Bros.) to the Frick Collection which states that the Frick pair came from the Wallace Collection (via the Wallaces' heir, Sir John Murray Scott). That the Frick pair was indeed modelled upon the Petworth commode (to the order of Lord Hertford in 1853) is argued convincingly in Hughes 2007, op. cit., pp.195–203. Hughes's thesis is strengthened considerably by the fact that the Frick copies and the Petworth commodes are linked by identical veined red marble tops, different in design to the Versailles tops supplied by Boulle (a fact not mentioned in the Frick catalogue).

272 Wallace Collection Archives 15L. The bill is quoted *in extenso* in P.Hughes, 'Replicas of French Furniture made for the 4th Marquess of Hertford,' *Antologia di Belle Arti*, 31–32, 1987, p.54. See also P.Hughes, *The Wallace Collection: Catalogue of Furniture*, 3 vols, London, 1996, vol. I, pp.31–32.

273 For the 18th-century versions of Boulle's Versailles commodes, see D.Dubon and T.Dell, *The Frick Collection, An Illustrated Catalogue, vol. V, Furniture: Italian and French*, New York, 1992, pp.233–46 (entry by Theodore Dell) and Hughes 2007 and 2008b.

274 For the later copies, see Dubon and Dell, ibid., and Hughes 2007, pp.201–02.

275 Hughes 2008a, pp.63–4 and fig.3.

276 Ibid., p.64 and fig.4; for the Boughton clock, see Tessa Murdoch, ed., *Boughton House: The English Versailles*, London, 1992, p.122, fig.114.

277 For an account of Lord and Lady Leconfield at Petworth, see Rowell 1997, especially pp.90–92.

278 For the Mentmore collection and an account of its formation, see the series of sale catalogues (Sotheby's, 18–20 May 1977), with a historical introduction by Sir Francis [F.J.B.] Watson, 'Mentmore and its Art Collections'.

279 W.S Lewis, ed., op. cit., vol.IX, p.97 (letter to George Montagu, dated 26 August 1749).

280 W.Cobbett, *Rural Rides*, G.Cole, ed., London, 1930, vol.I, p.335 (13 November 1825).

281 L. Simond, *Journal of a Tour and Residence in Great Britain*, Edinburgh, 1817, 2nd edn., vol.II, pp.326–7.

282 Leconfield 1938, p.44.

283 Egremont 1968, p.58.

284 Gore 1977b, p. 381.

Bibliography

The Petworth House Archives, which belong to Lord Egremont, are in the care of the West Sussex Record Office (a catalogue, so far comprising four volumes, has been published – in 1968, 1980, 1997 and 2003; a fifth is available online; a list of papers is available online at www.westsussexpast.org.uk/searchonline). An entire issue of *Apollo* (vol.CV, May 1977) was devoted to Petworth, with articles on the building, sculpture, furniture, paintings, garden and park. For the last, see also *Petworth Park and Pleasure Grounds: Historical Survey following the Great Storm of October 1987*, unpublished report (NT archive) funded by the National Heritage Memorial Fund.

ATTERBURY 1989
Atterbury, Paul, 'Hue and Cry', *Country Life*, 9 March 1989, pp.166–7 [Conservation of Antique sculpture at Petworth].

BATHO 1956
Batho, G.R., 'The Wizard Earl in the Tower', *History Today*, vol.VI, no.5, May 1956, pp.344–51.

BATHO 1957
Batho, G.R., 'The Percies at Petworth, 1574–1632', *Sussex Archaeological Collections*, vol.XCV, 1957, pp.1–27.

BATHO 1958
Batho, G.R., 'Notes and Documents on Petworth House, 1574–1632', *Sussex Archaeological Collections*, vol.XCVI, 1958, pp.108–34.

BATHO 1960
BATHO, G.R., 'The Library of the "Wizard" Earl: Henry Percy, Ninth Earl of Northumberland (1564–1632)', *The Library*, vol.XV, no.4, December 1960, pp.246–61.

BATHO 1962
Batho, G.R., ed., *The Household Papers of Henry Percy, Ninth Earl of Northumberland (1564–1632)*, Camden Third Series, vol.XCIII, Royal Historical Society, London, 1962, pp.112–30.

BINNEY 1973
Binney, Marcus, 'Petworth Park in Danger', *Country Life*, 6 September 1973, pp.620–1.

BLUNT 1980
Blunt, Anthony, 'Petworth Rehung', *National Trust Studies*, 1980, pp.110–32.

BRENAN 1902
Brenan, Gerald, *A History of the House of Percy: From the Earliest Times Down to the Present Century*, London, 1902.

BURNSTOCK 1993
Burnstock, Aviva, et al., 'Three Le Nain Paintings Re-examined', *The Burlington Magazine*, vol.CXXXV, October 1993, pp.678–87.

BUTLIN, LUTHER AND WARRELL 1989
Butlin, Martin, Luther, Mollie, and Warrell, Ian, *Turner at Petworth: Painter and Patron*, London, 1989.

CATOR 1993
Cator, Charles, 'Haupt at Petworth', *Furniture History*, vol.XXIX, 1993, pp.72–9.

COLLINS BAKER 1920
Collins Baker, C.H., *Catalogue of the Petworth Collection of Pictures in the Possession of Lord Leconfield*, London, 1920.

DAKERS 1993
Dakers, Caroline, *Clouds: The Biography of a Country House*, London, 1993.

DE FONBLANQUE 1887
De Fonblanque, Edward Barrington, *Annals of the House of Percy: from the conquest to the opening of the nineteenth century*, London, 1887.

EGREMONT 1968
Egremont, Lord [John Wyndham, 1st Lord Egremont and 6th Lord Leconfield], *Wyndham and Children First*, London, 1968.

EGREMONT 1985
Egremont, Max [2nd Lord Egremont and 7th Lord Leconfield] 'The Third Earl of Egremont and his Friends', *Apollo*, vol.CXXII, October 1985, pp.280–7.

ELLIS 1981
Ellis, Myrtle, 'The Egremont Plate at Petworth House', *Apollo*, vol.CXIII, April 1981, pp.240–3.

GARNETT 2004
Garnett, M., 'Wyndham, John Edward Reginald, first Baron Egremont and sixth Baron Leconfield (1920–1972)', *Oxford Dictionary of National Biography*, online edn, Oxford University Press, September 2004.

GILBERT 1978
Gilbert, Christopher, *The Life and Work of Thomas Chippendale, London*, 1978 (two vols.), vol.I, pp.282–6 [where the 3rd Earl of Egremont's account with Chippendale (PHA 6611) is published in full].

GORE 1977A
Gore, St John, 'Three Centuries of Discrimination' [the Petworth Picture Collection], *Apollo*, vol.CV, May 1977, pp.346–57.

GORE 1977B
Gore, St John, 'A Route of Ignominy' [the bypass threat to Petworth Park], *Apollo*, vol.CV, May 1977, pp.380–1.

GORE 1989
Gore, St John, 'Old Masters at Petworth', in *The Fashioning and Functioning of the British Country House*, G. Jackson-Stops, ed., *Studies in the History of Art 25*, National Gallery of Art, Washington, DC, 1989, pp.121–31.

GUILDING 2000
Guilding, Ruth, 'The 2nd Earl of Egremont's sculpture gallery at Petworth: A Plan by Charles Townley', *Apollo*, vol.CLI, April 2000, pp.27–29.

HALL 1993
Hall, Michael, 'Petworth House, Sussex', *Country Life*, 10 June 1993, pp.128–33.

HARRIS 1997
Harris, John, 'Recreating Petworth: New Evidence of its Original Appearance', *Apollo*, vol.CXLV, April 1997, pp.13–15.

HUGHES 2007
Hughes, Peter, 'The Grand Trianon Commodes by André-Charles Boulle and their Influence', *Furniture History*, vol.XLIII, 2007, pp.195–203.

HUGHES 2008A
Hughes, Peter, 'French Fashion at Petworth', *Apollo*, vol.CLXVIII, December 2008, pp.59–63.

HUGHES 2008B
Hughes, Peter, 'French Furniture at Petworth: Boulle and the Acquisitions from Hamilton Palace in 1882', *Apollo (National Trust Historic Houses and Collections Annual 2008)*, pp.58–66.

HUSSEY 1926
Hussey, Christopher, *The Story of Petworth House: Its Owners, Its Contents*, 1926 [reprinted from *Country Life* articles, 28 November, 5, 12, 19 December 1925, and 13 February 1926].

HUSSEY 1947
Hussey, Christopher, 'Petworth House, Sussex', *Country Life*, 7 March 1947, pp.422–5.

JACKSON-STOPS 1973
Jackson-Stops, Gervase, 'Petworth and the Proud Duke', *Country Life*, 28 June 1973, pp.1870–4.

JACKSON-STOPS 1975
Jackson-Stops, Gervase, 'Wilderness to Pleasure Ground: A New Threat to Petworth Park, Sussex', *Country Life*, 26 June 1975, pp.1686–7.

JACKSON-STOPS 1977A
Jackson-Stops, Gervase, 'The Building of Petworth', *Apollo*, vol.CV, May 1977, pp.24–33.

JACKSON-STOPS 1977B
Jackson-Stops, Gervase, 'Furniture at Petworth', *Apollo*, vol.CV, May 1977, pp.358–66.

JACKSON-STOPS 1980A
Jackson-Stops, Gervase, 'Bordering on Works of Art: Picture Frames at Petworth', *Country Life*, 4 September 1980, pp.798–800.

JACKSON-STOPS 1980B
Jackson-Stops, Gervase, 'Great Carvings for a Connoisseur: Picture Frames at Petworth', *Country Life*, 25 September 1980, pp.1031–2.

JACKSON-STOPS 1984
Jackson-Stops, Gervase, 'Rococo Masterpiece Restored: The Petworth State Bed', *Country Life*, 14 June 1984, pp.1698–700.

JACKSON-STOPS 1985
Jackson-Stops, Gervase, ed., *The Treasure Houses of Britain: Five Hundred Years of Private Patronage and Art Collecting*, exh. cat., National Gallery of Art, Washington, DC, Washington 1985 [numerous loans from Petworth].

JOLL 1977
Joll, Evelyn, 'Painter and Patron: Turner and the 3rd Earl of Egremont', *Apollo*, vol.CV, May 1977, pp.374–9.

KENWORTHY-BROWNE 1973
Kenworthy-Browne, John, 'Lord Egremont and

His Sculptors: The Collection at Petworth House, Sussex', *Country Life*, 7 June 1973, pp.1640–1.

KENWORTHY-BROWNE 1977
Kenworthy-Browne, John, 'The Third Earl of Egremont and Neo-Classical Sculpture', *Apollo*, vol.CV, May 1977, pp.367–73.

KLINGE 1991
Klinge, Margret, *David Teniers the Younger*, Ghent, 1991.

KNOX 2007
Knox, Tim, 'Petworth's Carved Room', *Country Life*, 15 February 2007, pp.68–71.

LAING 1995
Laing, Alastair, *In Trust for the Nation: Paintings from National Trust Houses*, exh. cat., The National Gallery, London, 1995.

LAING 2001A AND B
Laing, Alastair [entries on 'Egremont, third Earl of' and 'Petworth'], in *The Oxford Companion to J.M.W. Turner*, Evelyn Joll, Martin Butlin, & Luke Herrmann, eds., Oxford, 2001, pp.84–86 and 226–27.

LECONFIELD 1938
Leconfield, Constance, *Random Papers*, Southwick, 1938.

MCEVANSONEYA 2001
McEvansoneya, Philip, 'Lord Egremont and Flaxman's "St Michael overcoming Satan"', *The Burlington Magazine*, vol.CXLIII, June 2001, pp.351–9.

MACLEOD AND ALEXANDER 2007
Macleod, Catherine, and Alexander, Julia Marciari, 'The "Windsor Beauties" and the Beauties Series in Restoration England', *Politics, Transgression, and Representation at the Court of Charles II*, Paul Mellon Centre for Studies in British Art, 2007, pp.81–120.

MCCANN 1983
McCann, Alison, 'A Private Laboratory at Petworth House, Sussex, in the Late Eighteenth Century', *Annals of Science*, vol.XL, November 1983, pp.635–55.

MILLER 1975
Miller, Edward, 'A Collection of Elizabethan and Jacobean Plays at Petworth', *National Trust Studies*, 1975, pp.62–64.

MUSSON 2005
Musson, Jeremy, 'Turner's Bedroom Secrets', *Country Life*, 24 November 2005, p.64.

NORTHUMBERLAND 1770
Northumberland, Henry Algernon Percy, Earl of, *The Regulations and Establishment of the Household of Henry Algernon Percy, the Fifth Earl of Northumberland, at his Castles of Wresill and Lekinfield in Yorkshire. Begun Anno Domini M.DXII*, London, 1770. The preface is signed T.P (Thomas Percy, Bishop of Dromore), whose name also appears on the 1827 and the 1905 editions.

OLIVIER 1945
Olivier, Edith, *Four Victorian Ladies of Wiltshire*, Faber, London, 1945, pp.85–101 [Hon. Mrs Percy (Madeline) Wyndham].

PROUDFOOT AND ROWELL 1997
Proudfoot and Rowell, Trevor Proudfoot and Christopher Rowell, 'The Display and Conservation of Sculpture at Petworth', in Phillip Lindley, ed., *Sculpture conservation: preservation or interference?*, Ashgate, 1997, pp.179–193.

RAEDER, ERHARDT AND EDER 2000
Raeder, Joachim, Erhardt, Norbert, and Eder, Christian, *Die antiken Skulpturen in Petworth House (West Sussex)* in *Corpus signorum imperii Romani, Great Britain*, vol.III, *Monumenta artis Romanae: Antike Skulpturen in englischen Schlössern*, vol.XXVIII, (Philipp von Zabern), 2000.

ROWELL 1993
Rowell, Christopher, 'The North Gallery at Petworth: An Historical Re-appraisal', *Apollo*, vol.CXXXVIII, July 1993, pp.29–36.

ROWELL 1997
Rowell, Christopher, *Petworth House*, London, 1997 (and subsequent editions).

ROWELL 1998
Rowell, Christopher, 'The 2nd Earl of Egremont and Egremont House: A Private London Palace and its Pictures', *Apollo*, vol.CXLVII, April 1998, pp.15–21.

ROWELL 2000
Rowell, Christopher, 'Grinling Gibbon's Carved Room at Petworth: "The Most Superb Monument of his Skill"', *Apollo*, vol.CLI, April 2000, pp.19–26.

ROWELL 2002
Rowell, Christopher, 'Turner at Petworth: The 3rd Earl of Egremont's Carved Room Restored', *Apollo*, vol.CLV, 2002, pp.40–7.

ROWELL, WARRELL AND BLAYNEY BROWN 2002
Rowell, Christopher, Warrell, Ian, and Blayney Brown, David, *Turner at Petworth*, exh. cat. (Petworth House), London, 2002.

ROWELL 2003
Rowell, Christopher, '"Reigning toasts": Portraits of Beauties by Van Dyck and Dahl at Petworth', *Apollo*, vol.CLVII, April 2003, pp.39–47.

ROWELL 2004
Rowell, Christopher, 'Wyndham, George O'Brien, third earl of Egremont (1751–1837)' in H.C.G. Matthew and Brian Harrison, eds., *The Oxford Dictionary of National Biography*, Oxford, 2004 (and *DNB* online)

ROWELL 2010
Rowell, Christopher, 'New Light on Petworth's Louis XIV Table', *National Trust online arts | buildings | collections Bulletin*, Summer Issue, July 2010, p.12.

STEER 1955
Steer, F. W, 'Heraldic glass in the Percy chapel at Petworth House', *Journal of the British Society of Master Glass-Painters*, vol.XI, no.4, 1955, pp.213–20.

STROUD 1997
Stroud, Dorothy, 'The Gardens and Park', *Apollo*, vol.CV, May 1977, pp.334–9.

THOMAS 2002
Thomas, S., 'Power, Paternalism, Patronage and Philanthropy: The Wyndhams and the New Poor Law in Petworth,' *Local Historian*, vol.XXXII, no.2, 2002, pp.99–117.

VEGELIN VAN CLAERBERGEN 2006
Vegelin Van Claerbergen, Ernst, ed., *David Teniers and the Theatre of Painting*, London, 2006.

VERMEULE 1977
Vermeule, Cornelius, 'The Ancient Marbles at Petworth', *Apollo*, vol.CV, May 1977, pp.340–5.

WAAGEN 1854
Waagen, Gustav, *Treasures of Art in Great Britain*, London, 1854, vol.III, pp.31–43.

WALLIS 1951
Wallis, Helen, 'The First English Globe: A Recent Discovery', *Geographical Journal*, vol.CXVII, no.3, September 1951, pp.275–290.

WEBSTER 2007
Webster, Sarah, 'Estate Improvement and the Professionalisation of Land Agents on the Egremont Estates in Sussex and Yorkshire, 1770–1835', *Rural History*, vol. XVIII, no.1, 2007, pp.47–70.

WOOD 1993
Wood, Jeremy, 'The Architectural Patronage of Algernon Percy, 10th Earl of Northumberland', in *English Architecture Public and Private*, John Bold and Edward Chaney, eds., London, 1993, pp.55–80.

WOOD 1994
Wood, Jeremy, 'Van Dyck and the Earl of Northumberland: Taste and Collecting in Stuart England', in *Van Dyck 350*, S.Barnes and A. Wheelock, eds., *Studies in the History of Art 46*, National Gallery of Art, Washington, DC, 1994, pp.281–324.

WYNDHAM 1950
Wyndham, Hugh, *A Family History 1688–1837: The Wyndhams of Somerset, Sussex and Wiltshire*, London, 1950.

WYNDHAM 1915
Wyndham, Margaret, *Catalogue of the Collection of Greek and Roman Antiquities in the Possession of Lord Leconfield*, London, 1915.

YOUNGBLOOD 1983
Youngblood, Patrick, 'That House of Art: Turner at Petworth', *Turner Studies*, vol.II, no.2, 1983, pp.16–33.

Index

Figures in **bold** indicate captions.